T0193758

Isaiah 26:3–4
"PERFECT PEACE XIV"

G - Men

VANESSA RAYNER

authorHOUSE®

AuthorHouse™
1663 Liberty Drive
Bloomington, IN 47403
www.authorhouse.com
Phone: 1 (800) 839-8640

Published by AuthorHouse   05/01/2018

ISBN: 978-1-5462-4047-1 (sc)
ISBN: 978-1-5462-4046-4 (e)

Library of Congress Control Number: 2018905304

Print information available on the last page.

Contents

Theme vii
Prayer ix
Author's Notes xi
Preface xix
Thanks xxi
Acknowledgements.. xxiii
Introduction.. xxv
Dedication xxvii

Chapter 1   The List... 1
Chapter 2   Only Once.. 6
Chapter 3   Two or Three Times.......................... 13
Chapter 4   Four or Five Times............................ 17
Chapter 5   Six or Seven Times........................... 24
Chapter 6   Gaal and Gera 28
Chapter 7   Gershom and Gershon 32
Chapter 8   69 38
Chapter 9   Gedaliah and Gehazi 49
Chapter 10   The Mighty Warrior.......................... 56
Chapter 11   New Testament Only......................... 69
Chapter 12   A Specific Bible Book........................ 71
Chapter 13   One Chapter.................................... 73

A Reader's Question.. 77
Author's Closing Remarks 79
References 81
Answers & Information Section 83
Other Books by the Author:................................. 85

A Gift . . .

Presented to

_____

From

_____

Date

_____

Go in God's Presence with Expectation

Theme

The message of **I**saiah **26:3-4** is *"Perfect Peace."* This is the distinct and unifying composition of this book with the subtitle *G – Men*.

A Song of Praise

You will keep in perfect peace all who trust in you,
all whose thoughts are fixed on you!
Trust in the Lord always,
for the Lord God is the eternal Rock.
Isaiah 26:3-4 NLT

PS: Isaiah 26 has 21 verses, and is considered "A Song of Praise."

Prayer

Oh, Heavenly Father,
I thank you for another day, and another
opportunity to write another book.
I pray that your people are prospering
daily in their spirit, soul, and body
by reading, Perfect Peace Books.

Oh, Heavenly Father,
I ask in Jesus' name that the Holy Spirit will
help readers to remember Your word.
I pray it will give them peace, and joy,
at a time they need it the most.
I thank You for blessing those that
help Your work go forth.

Oh, Heavenly Father,
You have made it clear that You will reward
those that bless your servant.
It could be through prayer, words of encouragement,
to giving that person a cup of water.

Oh, Heavenly Father,
I give you all the Glory, Honor and Praise in Jesus' name.

Amen.

Author's Notes

Author notes generally provide a way to add extra information to one's book that may be awkward and inappropriate to include in the text of the book itself. It offers supplemental contextual details on the aspects of the book. It can help readers understand the book content and the background details of the book better. The times and dates of researching, reading, and gathering this information are not included; mostly when I typed on it.

0634; Sunday, 05 November 2017; Woke up this morning with this tune on my mind, "Precious Lord Take My Hand and Lead Me On." While making coffee, my inner spirit is urging me to write about the G – Men in the Bible. Hallelujah!

0141; Friday, 10 November 2017; Just woke up with a burning desire to write. Glory be to God.

0451; Saturday, 11 November 2017; Happy Veteran Day!

0626; Sunday, 12 November 2017

0736; Saturday, 18 November 2017

0428; Sunday, 19 November 2017

0735; Friday, 24 November 2017

0513, Saturday, 25 November 2017

1721; Thursday, 30 November 2017

1729; Friday, 01 December 2017

0611; Saturday, 02 December 2017

1536; Monday, 04 December 2017

1739; Thursday, 07 December 2017

0053; Saturday, 09 December 2017

0643; Sunday, 10 December 2017

1630; Monday, 11 December 2017

1853; Tuesday, 12 December 2017

1808; Thursday, 14 December 2017

0627; Saturday, 16 December 2017

0045; Sunday, 17 December 2017

1408; Monday, 18 December 2017; Earlier today at my Doctor Appointment, I was advised that the test results from Baptist East MRI of my brain were normal. Praise God! Just finished speaking with AuthorHouse Publishing Services Associate A.E. concerning a few changes to Isaiah 26:3-4 "Perfect Peace XIII" 1 Kings 19:1-18.

1546; Tuesday, 19 December 2017

1827; Thursday, 21 December 2017

0553; Saturday, 23 December 2017

0557; Sunday, 24 December 2017

0723; Monday, 25 December 2017; Merry Christmas

0629; Tuesday, 26 December 2017

0646; Sunday, 31 December 2017; Praise God Saints! I had a minor eye abrasion which causes me to visit Dr. F. Everson. Even though, I couldn't read or type about Father's word; I meditated on the Lord Prayer, Psalms 23, Ephesians 6, Galatians 5, Sermon on the Mount by Jesus, Ecclesiastes 3, The Books of the Bible, My Saviour's Disciples, and visit several telephones pray lines. Hallelujah! My left eye feels and looks much better, it still a little reddish, but at this moment it feels super strong. Shatopmama! Hallelujah, Lord, I Bless Your Holy Name!

0647; Monday, 02 January 2018; A New Year, Lord I thank You!

1656; Wednesday, 03 January 2018

1700; Thursday, 04 January 2018

0146; Saturday, 06 January 2018

1646; Tuesday, 09 January 2018

1710; Wednesday, 10 January 2018

2031; Friday, 12 January 2018; Just got off the <u>Breaking Bread Word Fellowship Prayer Line</u> where Pastor JoAnn is the host. Great message by Minister April from James 2.

0649; Sunday, 14 January 2018

0623; Monday, 15 January 2018; Martin Luther King Day

0916; Tuesday, 16 January 2018; Snowed in today, Memphis, Tn.

0621; Saturday, 20 January 2018

1632; Tuesday, 23 January 2018

1528; Wednesday, 24 January 2018

1656; Friday, 26 January 2018

0802; Saturday, 27 January 2018

0554; Sunday, 28 January 2018

1642; Monday, 29 January 2018

1713; Tuesday, 30 January 2018

1426; Wednesday, 31 January 2018

0605; Sunday, 04 February 2018

0637; Saturday, 10 February 2018

0013; Monday, 12 February 2018

1624; Tuesday, 13 February 2018

1638; Wednesday, 14 February 2018; Happy Valentine Day!

1825; Thursday, 15 February 2018

0653; Friday, 16 February 2018

0812; Saturday, 17 February 2018

0939; Sunday,18 February 2018

1741; Tuesday, 20 February 2018

1808; Wednesday, 21 February 2018

1648; Thursday, 22 February 2018

1840; Friday, 23 February 2018

0712; Saturday, 24 February 2018

1601; Monday, 26 February 2018

1701; Tuesday, 27 February 2018

0414; Wednesday, 28 February 2018; I can't sleep.

1700; Thursday, 01 March 2018

2236; Friday, 02 March 2018

0000; Saturday, 03 March 2018

0527; Sunday, 04 March 2018

1731; Wednesday, 07 March 2018

1802; Thursday, 08 March 2018

0747; Saturday, 10 March 2018

1831, Monday, 12 March 2018

1050; Wednesday, 14 March 2018; What a Mighty God we serve! Just got home from court, while I was setting there around 0921, I heard a still, small voice says "1129." I just smiled to myself, and asked Father God, "What can I relate "1129" to in the Bible?" I'm sure it will be revealed in God's timing. Now, I got get ready for work.

1826; Thursday, 15 March 2018

2147; Saturday, 17 March 2018

0730; Sunday, 18 March 2018

1924; Monday, 19 March 2018

2226; Tuesday, 20 March 2018

2223; Wednesday, 21 March 2018

2030; Thursday, 22 March 2018

1653; Friday, 23 March 2018

2034; Saturday, 24 March 2018; Attended Prophet Daniel Morris' twin sister funeral; "Danielle Morris." *~Absent from the Body, Present with The Lord~*

1910; Monday, 26 March 2018

1905; Tuesday, 27 March 2018; -323- Hallelujah!

1643; Wednesday, 28 March 2018

1822; Friday, 30 March 2018; Good Friday

0923; Saturday, 31 March 2018; I'm going do a little proofreading, before I leave for my tax appointment. "Shamorshekey," Lord I Praise Your Name, Lord, I Praise Your Name! Hallelujah . . .

0606; Sunday, 01 April 2018; Happy Easter

1912; Tuesday, 03 April 2018

1651; Wednesday, 04 April 2018

1732; Wednesday, 25 April 2018; Preparing to send manuscript to AuthorHouse.

Preface

Isaiah 26:3-4, "Perfect Peace XIV" ~ G – Men

The book Isaiah 26:3-4, "Perfect Peace XIV" G – Men is the 14th book in a series called Isaiah 26:3-4, "Perfect Peace." Hallelujah!

It all started from how I drew near to the LORD in my workplace by keeping my mind on Him. I related numbers, you see throughout the day, everywhere, on almost everything on Him, His word, biblical events, and facts to give me peace in the midst of chaos.

It's our desire for you to discover the power of the Holy Spirit by numbers, words, places, people, and things related to the "G – Men" in the Bible.

Remember, the LORD Jesus PROMISED us tribulation while we were in this world.

These things, I have spoken unto you,
that in me ye might have peace.
In the world ye shall have tribulation:
But be of good cheer; I have overcome the world.
John 16:33 KJV

However, we have been PROMISED His peace while we endure these trials, tribulations, troubles, and tests. Perfect Peace is given only to those whose mind and heart reclines upon the LORD. God's peace is increased in us according to the knowledge of His Holy Word.

> *Grace and peace be multiplied unto you*
> *through the knowledge of God,*
> *and of Jesus our LORD.*
> 2 Peter 1:2 KJV

Thanks

To the Readers . . .

As a disciple of the LORD Jesus Christ, I have learned true success comes when we are seeking and striving to do God's purpose for our lives. Our real happiness lies in doing God's will; not in fame and fortune.

Thank you for your support. Thank you for helping me spread "Perfect Peace" through your e-mail, Facebook, Twitter, LinkedIn, Instagram, Tumblr, Messenger and etc. accounts to your family, friends, neighbors, co-workers, church family, internet social friends, and associates.

Remember, you may not know until you get to heaven just how much a song you sung, kind words spoken by you or even a book you suggested reading, at the right moment, encourage a person to keep on going when a few minutes before they were tempted to give up on life and their walk with the LORD.

I greatly appreciate your love and kindness to this ministry.

Acknowledgements

First and foremost, I wish to express my sincere gratitude to *"Our Heavenly Father"* for his guidance, patience, and lovingkindness throughout the writing of this book.

I give my heartiest thanks to the following prayer lines. Even though, I didn't say much or visit every week, they allowed me to eat the crumbs that fall from their tables. Praise God!

Monday Nights	Bishop G. Coleman – <u>Without Boundaries Ministries</u>
Thursday/Saturday Nights	Prophet C.L. Allen – <u>End Time Prophetic Word</u>
Friday Nights	Pastor Jo Ann – <u>Breaking Bread Word Fellowship</u>
Sunday Nights	Elder Val – <u>International Faith Covenant Ministries</u>
Monday-Sunday	Pastor Donella Chambers

Introduction

For Those Who Want to Be Kept In "Perfect Peace"

This book was prepared and written to open your mind to a "Perfect Peace" that comes only from God. I'm striving to elevate you into a "Unique and Profound" awareness of God's presence around you at all time.

According to some people, it's hard to keep your mind on the LORD. While most Christians will agree that if you keep your mind stayed on the LORD, He will keep you in "Perfect Peace." This is why so many people enjoy going to church on Sundays and attending midweek services for peace and joy that they receive, but only for a short time.

You can experience the peace of the LORD throughout the day and every day. His unspeakable joy, his strength, his "Perfect Peace" in the midst of the storm whether it's at work, home, college, school, etc. You can also experience this peace, even when your day is going well.

This concept of this book was placed in my spirit by our Father, which art in heaven, to help me when he allowed Satan to test me at my workplace until he finished molding me into a MAP; (Minister/Ambassador/Pastor).

Throughout these pages, I will be focussing on biblical events, and facts surrounding the "G – Men" in the Bible. However, I am sure much more can be said concerning the "G – Men" in the Bible, so these subjects serve merely as an introduction and are not exhaustive by any means.

Dedication

This book is dedicated to . . . All the "G – Men" on the 7 continents of the world; Asia, Africa, North America, South America, Antarctica, Europe and Australia.

And especially my nephew, Grandville Broadway Jr.
June 1, 1974 – December 27, 1993
~ RIP ~

Note of Interests: The phrase "RIP" (Rest in Peace) comes from the Latin phrase "Requiescat in pace." It wishes the soul of a decedent eternal rest and peace in Christ. The phrase has been found in the catacombs of the early Christians that date back as far as 1st century BC.

Chapter 1

THE LIST

The names of the men in the Bible whose names begin with the letter "G" are listed below. I will call them "G – Men" of the Bible. The number inside the parenthesis indicates how many times that name is found in the King James Bible. Many of these names are mentioned only once, or twice, and several "G" names refer to more than one individual. How many can you say a few words about? Let's check them off.

__1. Gaal (9)   Judges 9:26   Judges 9:28   Judges 9:30

Judges 9:31   Judges 9:35   Judges 9:36

Judges 9:37   Judges 9:39   Judges 9:41

__2. Gabbai (1) Nehemiah 11:8

__3. Gad (69)   Genesis 30:11   Genesis 35:26   Genesis 46:16

Genesis 49:19   Exodus 1:4   Numbers 1:14

Numbers 1:24   Numbers 1:25   Numbers 2:14

Numbers 7:42   Numbers 10:20   Numbers 13:15

Numbers 26:15   Numbers 26:18   Numbers 32:1

Numbers 32:2   Numbers 32:6   Numbers 32:25

Numbers 32:29   Numbers 32:31   Numbers 32:33

Numbers 32:34   Numbers 34:14   Deuteronomy 27:13

Deuteronomy 33:20 Joshua 4:12   Joshua 13:24

Joshua 13:28   Joshua 18:7   Joshua 20:8

Joshua 21:7   Joshua 21:38   Joshua 22:9

Joshua 22:10   Joshua 22:11   Joshua 22:13

Joshua 22:15   Joshua 22:21   Joshua 22:25

Joshua 22:30	Joshua 22:31	Joshua 22:32
Joshua 22:33	Joshua 22:34	1 Samuel 13:7
1 Samuel 22:5	2 Samuel 24:5	2 Samuel 24:11
2 Samuel 24:13	2 Samuel 24:14	2 Samuel 24:18
2 Samuel 24:19	1 Chronicles 2:2	1 Chronicles 5:11
1 Chronicles 6:63	1 Chronicles 6:80	1 Chronicles 12:14
1 Chronicles 21:9	1Chronicles 21:11	1 Chronicles 21:13
1 Chronicles 21:18	1 Chronicles 21:19	1 Chronicles 29:29
2 Chronicles 29:25	Jeremiah 49:1	Ezekiel 48:27
Ezekiel 48:28	Ezekiel 48:34	Revelation 7:5

__4. Gaddi (1)   Numbers 13:11

__5. Gaddiel (1)   Numbers 13:10

__6. Gadi (2)   2 Kings 15:14   2 Kings 15:17

__7. Gaham (1)   Genesis 22:24

__8. Gahar (2)   Ezra 2:47   Nehemiah 7:49

__9. Gaius (5)   Acts 19:29   Acts 20:4   Romans 6:23
1 Corinthians 1:14   3 John 1:1

__10. Galal (3)   1 Chronicles 9:15   1 Chronicles 9:16   Nehemiah 11:17

__11. Gallio (3)   Acts 18:12   Acts 18:14   Acts 18:17

__12. Gamaliel (7)   Numbers 1:10   Numbers 2:20   Numbers 7:54
Numbers 7:59   Numbers 10:23   Acts 5:34
Acts 22:3

__13. Gamul (1)   1 Chronicles 24:17

__14. Gareb (3)   2 Samuel 23:38   1 Chronicles 11:40   Jeremiah 31:39

__15. Gashmu (4)   or Geshem   Nehemiah 2:19   Nehemiah 6:1
Nehemiah 6:2   Nehemiah 6:6

__16. Gatam (3)   Genesis 36:11   Genesis 36:16   1 Chronicles 1:36

__17. Gazez (2)   1 Chronicles 2:46

__18. Gazzam (2)   Ezra 2:48   Nehemiah 7:51

__19. Geber (2)   1 Kings 4:13   1 Kings 4:19

__20. Gedaliah (31)   2 Kings 25:22   2 Kings 25:23

2 Kings 25:24	2 Kings 25:25	1 Chronicles 25:3
1 Chronicles 25:9	Ezra 10:18	Jeremiah 38:1
Jeremiah 39:14	Jeremiah 40:5	Jeremiah 40:6
Jeremiah 40:7	Jeremiah 40:8	Jeremiah 40:9
Jeremiah 40:11	Jeremiah 40:12	Jeremiah 40:13
Jeremiah 40:14	Jeremiah 40:15	Jeremiah 40:16
Jeremiah 41:1	Jeremiah 41:2	Jeremiah 41:3
Jeremiah 41:4	Jeremiah 41:6	Jeremiah 41:9
Jeremiah 41:10	Jeremiah 41:16	Jeremiah 41:18
Jeremiah 43:6	Zephaniah 1:1	

___21. Gedor (7)

Joshua 15:58	1 Chronicles 4:4	1 Chronicles 4:18
1 Chronicles 4:39	1 Chronicles 8:31	1 Chronicles 9:37
1 Chronicles 12:7		

___22. Gehazi (12)

2 Kings 4:12	2 Kings 4:14	2 Kings 4:25
2 Kings 4:27	2 Kings 4:29	2 Kings 4:31
2 Kings 4:36	2 Kings 5:20	2 Kings 5:21
2 Kings 5:25	2 Kings 8:4	2 Kings 8:5

___23. Gemalli (1)   Numbers 13:12

___24. Gemariah (5)

Jeremiah 29:3	Jeremiah 36:10	Jeremiah 36:11
Jeremiah 36:12	Jeremiah 36:25	

___25. Genubath (1)   1 Kings 11:20

___26. Gera (9)

Genesis 46:21	Judges 3:15	2 Samuel 16:5
2 Samuel 19:16	2 Samuel 19:18	1 Kings 2:8
1 Chronicles 8:3	1 Chronicles 8:5	1 Chronicles 8:7

___27. Gershom (14)

	Exodus 2:22	Exodus 18:3
Judges 18:30	1 Chronicles 6:16	1 Chronicles 6:17
1 Chronicles 6:20	1 Chronicles 6:43	1 Chronicles 6:62
1 Chronicles 6:71	1 Chronicles 15:7	1 Chronicles 23:15
1 Chronicles 23:16	1 Chronicles 26:24	Ezra 8:2

___28. Gershon (18)

	Genesis 46:11	Exodus 6:16
Exodus 6:17	Numbers 3:17	Numbers 3:18

	Numbers 3:21	Numbers 3:25	Numbers 4:22
	Numbers 4:28	Numbers 4:38	Numbers 4:41
	Number 7:7	Numbers 10:17	Numbers 26:57
	Joshua 21:6	Joshua 21:27	1 Chronicles 6:1
	1 Chronicles 23:6		
__29. Gesham	or Geshan (1)	1 Chronicles 2:47	
__30. Gether (2)	Genesis 10:23	1 Chronicles 1:17	
__31. Geuel (1)	Numbers 13:15		
__32. Gibbar (1)	Ezra 2:20		
__33. Gibea (1)	1 Chronicles 2:49		
__34. Giddalti (2)	1 Chronicles 25:4	1 Chronicles 25:29	
__35. Giddel (4)	Ezra 2:47	Ezra 2:56	Nehemiah 7:49
	Nehemiah 7:58		
__36. Gideon (37)	Judges 6:11	Judges 6:13	Judges 6:19
	Judges 6:22	Judges 6:24	Judges 6:27
	Judges 6:29	Judges 6:34	Judges 6:36
	Judges 6:39	Judges 7:1	Judges 7:2
	Judges 7:4	Judges 7:5	Judges 7:7
	Judges 7:13	Judges 7:14	Judges 7:15
	Judges 7:18	Judges 7:19	Judges 7:20
	Judges 7:24	Judges 7:25	Judges 8:4
	Judges 8:7	Judges 8:11	Judges 8:13
	Judges 8:21	Judges 8:22	Judges 8:23
	Judges 8:24	Judges 8:27	Judges 8:28
	Judges 8:30	Judges 8:32	Judges 8:33
	Judges 8:35		
__37. Gideoni (5)	Numbers 1:11	Numbers 2:22	Numbers 7:60
	Numbers 7:65	Numbers 10:24	
__38. Gilalai (1)	Nehemiah 12:36		
__39. Ginath (2)	1 Kings 16:21	1 Kings 16:22	
__40. Ginnetho	or Ginnethon (3)	Nehemiah 12:4	Nehemiah 10:6

__41. Gispa	Nehemiah 12:16 or Gishpa (1)	Nehemiah 11:21	
__42. Goliath (6)	1 Samuel 17:4	1 Samuel 17:23	1 Samuel 21:9
	1 Samuel 22:10	2 Samuel 21:19	1 Chronicles 20:5
__43. Gomer (5)	Genesis 10:2	Genesis 10:3	1 Chronicles 1:5-6
	Ezekiel 38:6	Hosea 1:3	(Female named Gomer)
__44. Guni (4)	Genesis 46:24	Numbers 26:48	1 Chronicles 5:15
	1 Chronicles 7:13		

Hopefully, after you finish reading this book, you will be able to check off a few more. Enjoy!

Note of Interests: I could only speak on 9 out of 44 "G – Men." They are listed below with the first thing that popped into my mind about the name.

3. Gad – the son of Jacob by Rachel's maidservant, Bilhah

9. Gaius – a friend of Paul

11. Gallio – dismissed charges in court against Paul by the Jews

12. Gamaliel – a teacher of the Apostle Paul

22. Gehazi – Elisha's servant

27. Gershom – Moses' son

36. Gideon – Became a mighty warrior for the Lord

42. Goliath – David killed him with a sling and a stone

43. Gomer – I could only recall the female Gomer, the wife of Hosea who was unfaithful

~~~~~~~~~~~~

Chapter 2

ONLY ONCE

The "G – Men" named in this chapter only appear once in the Bible. The information surrounding their life and livelihood is brief. However, whether it's one sentence or a few more their names are written in the Bible.

Gabbai
Nehemiah 11:8

Nehemiah chapters 11 and 12 lists the names of the Jewish people who repopulated Jerusalem, after being released from the Babylonian captivity. The rulers and leaders of the people dwelt in Jerusalem, while the rest of the people cast lots to choose one individual out of ten to come and live in the holy city; Jerusalem. The other nine individuals would remain in their cities, towns, and villages.

From the tribe of Benjamin, three leaders settled in Jerusalem. The first was Sallu, son of Meshullam, and the others were Gabbai and Sallai. Sallu's ancestors were Joed, Pedaiah, Kolaiah, Maaseiah, Ithiel, and Jeshaiah, a total of 928 people. Joel, son of Zikri, was their leader, and Judah, son of Hassenuah was second in command. Gabbai was one of the leaders of the tribe of Benjamin, according to Nehemiah 11:8. The chapter also lists the names of the priests, the Levites, temple guards and others that settled in Jerusalem.

Gaddi
Numbers 13:11

The Wilderness of Paran is one of the places where the Israelites spent part of their 40 years of wandering after the Exodus. They arrived in the Wilderness of Paran after a three-day journey north of Mount Sinai. It was from Kadesh in Paran that twelve spies were sent into the Promised Land to gather information.

Gaddi was among the twelves spies sent by Moses from the Wilderness of Paran to spy out the land of Canaan before Israel conquest around 1490 BC. Gaddi was from the tribe of Manasseh, the son of Susi. He was considered one of the chiefs of the tribe of Manasseh. The name Gaddi means "my troop," and it's pronounced "Ga-di."

The Wilderness of Paran is also called the Desert of Paran. It was the home of Ishmael, Genesis 21:8-21. A place where David took refuge from Saul, and where he married Abigail, the widow of Nabal, 1 Samuel 25.

Gaddiel
Numbers 13:10

Gaddiel was one of the twelve spies sent by Moses to spy out the land of Canaan. After 40 days, the spies returned. He was one of the ten men who came back expressing doubt that they could conquer the people of the land that was living there, Numbers 14:37. Caleb and Joshua were the only two who believed they could conquer the land. However, the majority prevailed, and Israel wandered in the wilderness another 38 years until that entire generation died.

Gaddiel, the son of Sodi, was from the tribe of Zebulun, and a chief of the tribe. Zebulun was the 10th son of Jacob's 12 sons, the 6th and last son of his 1st wife, Leah. The name of Gaddiel means "God is my fortune," and it's pronounced "Gad-dee-el."

Gaham
Genesis 22:24

This G-man is listed as the 2nd son of Nahor. Remember, Nahor was Abram (Abraham) brother. Gaham's mother was named Reumah, a concubine who had three more sons with his father, and their names were Tebah, Thahash, and Maachah. His father Nahor had eight more sons with his wife, Milcah. The name "Gaham" means "to burn."

Note of Interests: Gaham's father Nahor married the daughter of his oldest brother, Haran. Her name was Milcah, and she was his niece, Genesis 11:29. They were born and raised in the ancient city Ur of the Chaldeans, in which this sort of marriage was allowed, as well as marriage between brothers and sisters, Exodus 6:20. Abraham was called by God to leave Ur of the Chaldeans, and to journey to a land that God would show him, Genesis 12:1-9. Afterward, it was strictly forbidden in the Levitical Laws to marriage family members, Leviticus 18:12-14.

~~~~~~~~~~~~

Gamul
1 Chronicles 24:17

Gamul was a descendant of Aaron, and he was also a priest and a chief of the Levites. The sons of Aaron were Nadab, Abihu, Eleazar, and Ithamar. The two eldest sons of Aaron died before they had any children; Nadab and Abihu. According to Leviticus 10, they offered a sacrifice to the Lord with "strange fire," by disobeying God's instructions, they were immediately consumed by God's fire. So only Eleazar and Ithamar were left to carry on as priests.

David divided the clans of Eleazar and Ithamar into 24 groups by casting lots to serve at various times in the House of the Lord. The 22nd lot fell to Gamul, who became the group leader during that period. Gamul served in the sanctuary during King David era. His name means "recompense."

Gemalli
Numbers 13:12

The name Gemalli means "camel owner." His name is pronounced "ge-mal I," and it occurs only once in the Bible. Gemalli was the father of Ammiel from the tribe of Dan, who joined the group of twelve spies that Moses sent to check out Canaan; the Promised Land. Gemalli was one of the ten spies who returned with a negative report, expressing doubt that they could conquer the people of the land that was living there, Numbers 14:37.

Genubath
1 Kings 11:20

Genubath's father Hadad was an Edomite, who was from the royal line in Edom. He fled to Egypt from Edom when it was invaded by David's army under the leadership of Joab, who proceeded to kill all the males of Edom.

Genubath's father Hadad found great favour before Pharaoh, the King of Egypt. He gave Hadad in marriage the sister of his own wife, Tahpenes. The sister of Queen Tahpenes bore Hadad, a son who was named Genubath. Genubath was raised in Pharaoh's palace among the sons of Pharaoh. Genubath name is pronounced "ge - nu – bath," and it means "theft."

Gesham or Geshan
1 Chronicles 2:47

The name "Gesham" is sometimes written "Geshan." He was a son of Jahdai, a descendant of Judah through Caleb. His brothers are Regem, Jotham, Pelet, Ephah, and Shaaph. Gesham name means "firm, strong," and it's pronounced "ge - shan." First Chronicles 1:1 begins the "Historical Records," and Gesham's name is listed in 1 Chronicles 2 under Judah with the subtitle The Clans of Caleb.

Geuel
Numbers 13:15

The Geuel name means "God's redemption." He was a prince of Gad and the representative of the Gadite tribe who was sent out to spy and explore Canaan with the eleven others. The name Geuel is pronounced "gih yoo' ehl."

Gibbar
Ezra 2:20

Gibbar is the father of some of the Jewish exiles who returned with Zerubbabel from Babylon. King Nebuchadnezzar had captured many of the people of Judah and deported them to Babylon as prisoners. After 70 years of captivity, they were allowed to return back to Jerusalem and the other towns where they initially lived. According to Ezra 2:20, the family of Gibbar returned with 95 members. His name means "strong, manly."

Gibea
1 Chronicles 2:49

One of Caleb's concubine name was Maacah. She was the mother of Sheber and Tirhanah. Maacah was also the mother of Shaaph and Sheva. Shaaph was Madmannah's father, and Sheva was the father of Macbenah and Gibea. Gibea is the grandson of Caleb. His name means "a hill."

Gilalai
Nehemiah 12:36

Gilalai was a Levite musician and priest at the consecration of the wall of Jerusalem. The people came from the nearby towns and villages to dedicate the new wall of Jerusalem around 446 BC. During the ceremony, the people were singing and praising God. They played the music of cymbals, harps, and lyres in the procession at the dedication. The Asaph's brothers played the musical instruments that David had made. Their names were Shemaiah, Azarel, Milalai, Gilalai, Maai, Nethanel, Judah and Hanani. Ezra the scribe led the group who were there to dedicate the wall. The name Gilalai means "a wheel," and it is pronounced "gil'-a-li."

Gispa or Gishpa
Nehemiah 11:21

Gispa was an overseer of the Nethinims in Nehemiah's era. Nethinim was the name given to the temple servants in ancient Jerusalem. The Nethinims dwelt in the hills of Ophel, and Gispa and Ziha were in charge of them, after the return from Babylonian captivity. The name Gispa is pronounced "ghish - paw," and it means "coming hither."

Chapter 3

TWO OR THREE TIMES

The names of these "G – Men" appear in the Bible two or three times. Some are mentioned in only one chapter of the Bible, two or three times. There are others who are mentioned two or three times in more than one chapter of the Bible. One G-man's name is the name of two men, and another is mentioned twice in one sentence.

Gadi
2 Kings 15:14
2 Kings 15:17

His name means "God is my fortune." Gadi was the father of King Menahem, the 16th King of Israel. He came up from Tirzah to Samaria and killed Shallum and succeeded him as king. Gadi's son, Menahem is listed as an evil king, who worshipped idols. King Menahem reigned over Israel for 10 years from Samaria.

Gahar
Ezra 2:47
Nehemiah 7:49

Gahar was one of the chiefs of the Nethinim families. His descendants returned to Jerusalem under Zerubbabel from Babylon captivity. His name means "hiding place," and is pronounced "ga-har."

Galal
1 Chronicles 9:15
1 Chronicles 9:16
Nehemiah 11:17

The name "Galal" means "a roll." Galal is the name of two Levites in the Bible. According to 1 Chronicles 9:15, one Levite was the son of Mika, the son of Zikri, the son Asaph; around 536 BC. The other Levite is from the family of Elkanah who lived in the "villages of the Netophathites," 1 Chronicles 9:16, and Nehemiah 11:17.

The "villages of the Netophathites" are mentioned as dwelling places for Levites, and sons of the singers. The total number of Levites living in these villages were 284. They were located about 3 miles south of Jerusalem and 3 ½ miles south of Bethlehem. Netophathites is named as the birthplace of two of David's mighty warriors named Maharai and Heleb, 2 Samuel 23:28-29.

Gallio
Acts 18:12
Acts 18:14
Acts 18:17

According to Acts 18, Paul went to Corinth, and he found a Jew named Aquila who had recently moved from Italy with his wife Priscilla because Emperor Claudius had commanded all the Jews to leave Rome. Paul stayed and worked with them because he earned his living making tents, just as they did. Paul spent his time preaching in the synagogue every Sabbath, trying to convince both Jews and Greeks that Jesus is the Messiah. Later, Paul left Aquila and Priscilla to stay with a Gentile named Titius Justus who worshiped God.

One night, Paul had a vision, and the Lord said to him, "Don't be afraid, keep on speaking and don't up, I am with you. Not a single person will be able to harm you, for many people in this city belongs to me." So, Paul stayed there for a 1 ½ years, teaching the people the word of God.

Junius Annaeus Gallio was the Roman proconsul of Achaia under emperor Claudius when Paul visited Corinth around 53 AD, Acts 18:12. He is spoken by his contemporaries as "sweet Gallio." He is described as an amiable, upright and affectionate man. When the Jews made an insurrection against Paul and brought him before the judgment seat, Gallio refused to listen to them or entertain their clamorous and unjust demands. Gallio had those Jews ejected from the court, Acts 18:16.

Gazez
1 Chronicles 2:46

Gazez is a name which occurs twice in one verse, 1 Chronicles 2:46. He is mentioned first as a son of Caleb by Ephah, his concubine, and then as the son of Haran, the son of the same woman. The second is believed by scholars to be a repetition of the first. Other scholars believe they were a son and a brother of Haran. Older commentators thought it to be a son and grandson of Caleb. The name means "shearer," and it's pronounced "gaw-zaze."

Ginnetho or Ginnethon
Nehemiah 10:6
Nehemiah 12:4
Nehemiah 12:16

The name Ginnetho means "Gardner." According to Nehemiah 10:6, Ginnetho was a companion of Nehemiah who went back to Jerusalem to rebuild the city for God. Ginnetho was a Levite, and one of the chief priest who returned to Judah from exile with Zerubbabel and the High Priest Joshua, Nehemiah 12. The name Ginnetho is also spelled "Ginnethon."

Chapter 4

FOUR OR FIVE TIMES

Gaius

The name Gaius is mentioned 5 times in the Bible and is shared by several men in the New Testament. It was a common name in the first century. These men were involved in the ministry of the Apostles in one way or another.

Gaius in Corinth: Paul baptized a man named Gaius in Corinth, 1 Corinthians 1:14. During the end of Paul 3rd missionary journey, he stayed in Gaius' home. When Paul wrote the Epistle to the Romans, Gaius is included in his greetings to the church in Rome, Romans 16:23.

Gaius of Macedonia: Luke identifies him as a Macedonian, Acts 19:29. He was one of Paul's traveling companions during his 3rd missionary journey, 52-56 AD. Paul and his companions, Gaius and Aristarchus, were preaching the word of God throughout the province of Asia. The people started believing in God, and stopped worshipping idols, and burnt them.

A great riot broke out in Ephesus led by Demetrius and other silversmiths who obtain their wealth by manufacturing silver shrines of the Greek goddess Artemis. The mob dragged Gaius to the Ephesians' court and would have done harm to him if it wasn't for the speech, and intervention of the city clerk, Acts 19:35-41.

<u>Gaius of Derbe</u>: He was another of Paul's traveling companions on his 3rd missionary journey. Luke calls him "Gaius from Derbe" in Acts 20:4. The city Derbe was a city in the Roman province of Galatia in Asia Minor. The phrase "Gaius from Derbe" was used to distinguish him from the Gaius mentioned in Acts 19, who was from Macedonia.

<u>Gaius, John's Dear Friend</u>: The book of 3rd John is a General Epistle written around 85 AD. It was addressed to a man named Gaius. Gaius was a member of an unnamed church that John was the overseer of, 3 John 1:1. Gaius is commended for his hospitality to traveling preachers of the gospel, his faithfulness, his love, and his walk in the truth, 3 John 1:1-14. According to tradition, this Gaius may be the one whom John appointed as Bishop of Pergamum. The name Gaius means "happy" or "one who rejoices."

Gashmu

Gashmu's name is mentioned 4 times in the Bible; once in Nehemiah 2 and thrice in Nehemiah 6. Gashmu is the Aramaic spelling of Geshem written in Nehemiah 6:6, KJV and ASV. He was one of the enemies of the Jews after their return from Babylonian captivity. Gashmu united with Sanballat, Tobiah, the Ammonites, along with the Ashdodites in opposing the rebuilding of the wall of Jerusalem.

Tobiah and Gashmu were regional governors serving under the king of Persia. Sanballat the Horonite was from a city of Moab. Tobiah the Ammonite was governing an area east of Jordan River, and Gashmu the Arab was probably over the region of south Judah.

Sanballat, Tobiah, and Geshem used various ploys in their attempt to disrupt the building of the wall of Jerusalem. According to Nehemiah 6:2, these three men sought to harm Nehemiah. They intimidate him with false reports, Nehemiah 6:5-6. They tried to deceive him with false prophets, Nehemiah 6:7-13. They influence the nobles of Judah, Nehemiah 6:17-19. The efforts of the three were futile for they were fighting God's plan. The wall of Jerusalem was completed in record time, Nehemiah 6:15.

Nehemiah's responded to his enemies by taking the matter to God, Almighty, Nehemiah 6:14.

Remember, O my God,
all the evil things that Tobiah and Sanballat have done.
And remember Noadiah the prophet
And all the prophets like her who
have tried to intimidate me.
Nehemiah 6:14 NIV

Note of Interests: Geshem is the only Arab person mentioned in the Bible.

~~~~~~~~~~~

Gemariah

The name Gemariah is mentioned 5 times in the Bible in the book of Jeremiah, but it applies to at least 2 individuals.

In Jeremiah 29, Gemariah, the son of Hilkiah and Elasah, the son of Shaphan were the bearer of a letter written by Jeremiah from Jerusalem to the Jewish captives in Babylon, 594 BC. Jeremiah's message warned the captive Jews against false prophets who promised them a speedy return back to Jerusalem. Jeremiah told them the Lord of Heaven, the God of Israel says to build homes, plant gardens, eat the food, marry, have children, and plan to stay. They will be in Babylon for 70 years, then God would bring them out as He had promised, Jeremiah 29:10.

The other Gemariah, according to Jeremiah 36:10 was one of the Levities of the temple in the time of Jehoiakim. Around 606 BC, Gemariah a noble of Judah had a chamber in the house of the Lord, from which Baruch read Jeremiah's alarming prophecy from a scroll in the ears of all the people. Hoping that they would stop sinning and turn back to God.

Baruch also read what was written on the scroll to the king's officials. Afterward, they decided the king needs to hear it, but they told Baruch that he and Jeremiah need to go into hiding. When Jehudi started reading the scroll to King Jehoiakim and his officials, every time Jehudi finished reading three or four columns from the scroll, the king would tell him to cut it from the parchment and throw it in the fire. Elnathan, Delaiah, and Gemariah begged the king not to burn the scroll, but he ignored them, Jeremiah

36:1-25. The name Gemariah means "perfection of the Lord."

Giddel

The name Giddel means "very great." It is mentioned 4 times in the Bible; twice in Ezra 2 and twice in Nehemiah 7. The name belongs to two men in the Bible. One was the leader of a group of Temple Servants who returned from Babylonian captivity with Zerubbabel. The word "Nethinim" was the name given to the Temple Servants in ancient Jerusalem. The children of Giddel were among the Nethinim who returned to Jerusalem, Ezra 2:47, Nehemiah 7:49.

The other Giddel is named Bene-Giddel who was listed among the "servants of Solomon" who returned to Judea, Ezra 2:56, Nehemiah 7:58.

Gideoni

Gideoni name is mentioned 5 times in the Bible, only in the book of Numbers. On the first day of the second month of the second year after Israel had departed from the land of Egypt, the Lord spoke to Moses in the "Tent of Meeting" in the Wilderness of Sinai. He told Moses to take a census of the entire Israelite community by their clans and families, listing every man by name.

One man from each tribe was to help Moses and Aaron conduct this census. Gideoni, the father of Abidan, was selected as one of the census-taker. He was also the leader of the people of Benjamin whose numbered total 35,400 people. The name Gideoni name means "a cutting down."

Gomer

The male Gomer's name is mentioned 5 times in the Bible. According to the Bible, Noah lived approximately 1,500 years after Creation. He is considered the 10th patriarch from the beginning of time. He lived to be 950 years old, Genesis 9:29. Noah had three sons, and their names were Shem, Ham, and Japheth. Gomer was the eldest son of Japheth. Gomer's brothers were Magog, Madai, Javan, Tubal, Meshech, and Tiras. Gomer was the father of Ashkenaz, Riphath, and Togarmah. He is the father of the ancient Cimmerians, who settled on the northern shores of the Black Sea. His descendants formed the principal branch of the population of South-eastern Europe. The name means "to finish."

Notes of Interests: Gomer is also the name of the wife of the prophet Hosea, Hosea 1. She was considered a "promiscuous woman," a "harlot," and a "whore" but Hosea is told to marry her by God, Hosea 1:2.

~~~~~~~~~~~~

Guni

Guni is mentioned 4 times in Bible genealogy. He was the second son of Naphtali, and the grandson of Jacob, Genesis 46:24, 1 Chronicles 7:13. Guni's brothers were Jahziel, Jezer, and Shillem. Guni's descendants are called Gunites, and he's a member of the tribe of Gad who settled in Gilead, Numbers 26:48. According to 1 Chronicles 5:15, Guni was the father of Abdiel and a Gadite chief. The name Guni means "painted."

Chapter 5

SIX OR SEVEN TIMES

Gamaliel (7)

Numbers 1:10	Numbers 2:20
Numbers 7:54	Numbers 7:59
Numbers 10:23	Acts 5:34
Acts 22:3	

Gamaliel is a Hebrew name, and it means "reward of God." There are possible two men named Gamaliel in the Bible. One was the captain of the tribe of Manasseh at the census at Sinai, Number 1:10, Numbers 2:20, Numbers 7:54, and Numbers 7:59.

The other Gamaliel is recognized as a 1st Century Jewish rabbi and a leader in the Jewish Sanhedrin. According to Acts 5, the meeting of the Sanhedrin is where Apostles John and Peter are standing trial. After they were warned to cease preaching in the name of Jesus. The Jewish council became infuriated when Simon Peter defiantly replies, "We must obey God rather than human beings!" Acts 5:29. Gamaliel was a man, held in high esteem by all Jews, who spoke not to condemn the Apostles of Jesus to death, Acts 5:34. Gamaliel was also the Jewish law teacher of "Saul of Tarsus" who later became known as "Paul the Apostle," Acts 22:3.

Gedor (7)

Joshua 15:58	1 Chronicles 4:4
1 Chronicles 4:18	1 Chronicles 4:39
1 Chronicles 8:31	1 Chronicles 9:37
1 Chronicles 12:7	

The name Gedor means "a fortress" or "a wall." This name is connected with several families and a city. According to 1 Chronicles 4:4, Penuel was called the father of Gedor, and Ezer, the father of Hushah, the descendants of Hur, the firstborn of Ephrathah and father of Bethlehem.

According to 1 Chronicles 4:18, Gedor is one of the children of Mered's wives. Mered's wife was from the tribe of Judah, and she gave birth to Jered, the father of Gedor, Heber, and Jekuthiel.

According to 1 Chronicles 8:29, 30, and 1 Chronicles 9:35, Jeiel the father of Gibeon lived in Gibeon. His wife was Maacah, and his firstborn son was Abdon. Jeiel other sons were Zur, Kish, Baal, Ner, Nadab, Gedor, Ahio, Zecher, and Mikloh. They were exiles who resettled in Jerusalem after being carried away to Babylon. According to 1 Chronicles 8:31 and 1 Chronicles 9:37, Gedor the son of Jeiel was a descendant of King Saul because Gedor's brother Ner begot Kish, and Kish begot Saul, and Saul begot Jonathan, etc.

According to 1 Chronicles 12:7, the sons of Jeroham from Gedor were named in the list of David's mighty warriors, who joined him at Ziklag. Gedor is also the name of a city that belongs to the tribe of Simeon. It's located in the hill country of Judah surrounded by rich pastures, previously occupied by the Amalekites, Joshua 15:58 and 1 Chronicles 4:39. The city of Gedor is now called Jedur.

Goliath (6)

1 Samuel 17:4	1 Samuel 17:23
1 Samuel 21:9	1 Samuel 22:10
2 Samuel 21:19	1 Chronicles 20:5

The name Goliath means "uncover, reveal." Goliath, the Gittite from Gath, was a giant soldier in the Philistine army that challenged the Israelite army. Scholars believe that he was a descended from the Rephaim. They found refuge among the Philistines after they were dispersed by the Ammonites, Deuteronomy 2:20-21.

Goliath terrorized King Saul and his army for 40 days. Saul and his army camped on one side of a mountain peak, while the Philistines camped on the other side, and a valley called Elah was between. Goliath, the warrior, would come out between the lines of war and challenged the Israelites to send out a warrior for single combat, twice a day; morning and evening.

Goliath would shout to the Israelites, if the man they send out to fight him, kills him, then the Philistines would be

Israel's servants. But if he prevails, and kills him, then Israel would serve the Philistines. When Saul and all Israel heard these words of the Philistine, they were dismayed and terrified.

Goliath stood over 9 feet tall. He wore a bronze helmet, had a bronze armor to protect his chest and legs. His chest armor weighted about 125 pounds. He carried a bronze sword strapped to his back, and his iron spearhead weighted more than 15 pounds. Goliath had a soldier that always walked in front of him to carry his shield.

Goliath was defeated by young David when he was about 15 years old in 1025 BC.

He was killed by David with a stone from his sling, 1 Samuel 17. David then cut off his head and brought it to Jerusalem. He hung Goliath's armor in his tent, 1 Samuel 17:51. Goliath's sword was preserved at Nob as a religious trophy, 1 Samuel 21:9. David's victory over Goliath labeled him as the deliverer of Israel, and he became the chief among Saul's men of war, 1 Samuel 18:5, and the devoted friend of Jonathan; Saul's son.

According to 1 Chronicles 20:5, war broke out with the Philistines again at Gob, and Elhanan, the son of Jair killed Lahmi, the brother of Goliath the Gittite.

Chapter 6

GAAL AND GERA

Gaal

The names Gaal and Gera are mentioned 9 times in the Old Testament, only. Gaal's name is found only in the book of Judges 9. It is mentioned 9 times between verses 26 – 41. He is the son of Ebed, in whom the Shechemites placed their confidence in when they rebelled against Abimelech.

Abimelech was the son of Gideon the judge and his father's concubine who lived in Shechem. After his father death around 1027 BC, he convinced the Shechemites to appoint him as his father's successor. Abimelech then killed all but one of his 70 brothers to eliminate competition. Jotham was the youngest brother, and he was the only one to escape Abimelech's wrath by fleeing to Beer.

Gaal headed a revolution and led the men of Shechem out to battle against Abimelech. Gaal had boasted to Zebul, the ruler of Shechem that he could defeat Abimelech. Zebul secretly warned Abimelech of Gaal plans and offered a way to defeat Gaal. Gaal was defeated by Abimelech and drove back to the gates of Shechem. Zebul consequently drove Gaal and his remaining kinsmen from Shechem altogether. Gaal is mentioned no more after this battle. The name Gaal means "loathing."

<u>Gera</u>

The name Gera means "a grain." It is found in several books of the Old Testament and is the name of several Israelites, and they are as follow.

1.   Genesis 46 lists the names of the sons of Israel who went to Egypt; Jacob and his sons, and son's families. The total household of Jacob who settled in Egypt was 70 in a land called Goshen. Gera was an individual named among the people of the tribe of Benjamin, Genesis 46:21. He was the sons of Benjamin, and his brothers were Belah, Becher, Ashbel, Naaman, Ehi, Rosh, Muppim, Huppim, and Ard.

2.   In Judges 3, the Bible speaks of Ehud the son of Gera, a Benjamite, a man who was lefthanded, Judges 3:15. The Lord raised Gera's son to deliverer Israel from King Eglon of Moab. The Israelites did evil in the eyes of the Lord, again. He gave Eglon king of Moab power over them for 18 years. When Israelites cried out to the Lord, he gave them a deliverer named Ehud, the son of Gera.

Ehud had made a double-edged sword, which he strapped to his right thigh under his clothing. The king of Moab was a very obese man. After Ehud presented the tribute, he sent on their way those who had carried it. Ehud went back to Eglon and told him he had a secret message for him. The king told his attendants, they could leave, and they left.

Ehud, the son of Gera, told the king he had a message from God. The king rose from his seat, and Ehud reached with his left hand, and drew the sword from his right thigh, then plunged it into the king's belly. Ehud did not pull the sword out, and the king's fat closed it. Ehud then went out on the porch, shut the doors of the upper room behind him and locked them.

Ehud escaped to Seirah, and when he arrived, he blew a trumpet in the hill of Ephraim, and the Israelites went down with him from the hills, with him leading the way. He told the men to follow him because the Lord has given Moab, their enemies into their hands. They followed him and took possession of the fords of the Jordan that led to Moab. They allowed no one to cross over, and the Israelites struck down 10,000 Moabites, and that day Moab was made subject to Israel, and the land had peace for 80 years, Judges 3:26-30.

3.   According to 2 Samuel 16, the 3rd Gera is the ancestor of Shimei who cursed David. When King David approached a village named Bahurim, a man from the family of the house of Saul, whose name was Shimei son of Gera, came out cursing continuously at David and his men.

Gera threw stones at David and all the king's officials, as well as the people and soldiers who were on David's right and left side. As Shimei yelled curses, he shouted, "Leave! Leave! You man of bloodshed, you wicked man! The Lord has punished you for all the spilled blood of the house of Saul, in whose place you rule. Now the Lord has given the kingdom into the hand of your son, Absalom. Disaster has overtaken you, for you are a man of bloodshed!"

Beginning in 2 Samuel 15, David's son, Absalom led a rebellion against him. A messenger arrived in Jerusalem to tell David, that all Israel has joined Absalom in a conspiracy against him. David and his men and followers hurried out the palace and city before Absalom arrives, so the city of Jerusalem would be spared from disaster, 2 Samuel 15:14.

As David and his men were fleeing, at the summit of the Mount of Olives, Ziba, the servant of Mephibosheth brought David 2 donkeys loaded with 200 loaves of bread, 100 clusters of raisins, 100 bunches of summer fruit, and a wineskin full of wine, 2 Samuel 16:1. When King David came to the village of Bahurim, the son of Gera, named Shimei cursed and threw stones at them, 2 Samuel 16:13.

Chapter 7

GERSHOM AND GERSHON

Gershom

The name Gershom is the name of several individuals in the Bible. It is mentioned 14 times in the King James Bible. According to Exodus 2:22, Exodus 18:3, 1 Chronicles 23:15, and 1 Chronicles 26:24, it's the name of Moses and Zipporah first-born son around 1530 BC.

Zipporah was the wife of Moses, and the daughter of Jethro, the priest of Midian. When Moses fled from Egypt, he met Jethro's seven daughters, who were having trouble getting water for their flocks, Exodus 2. The troughs for watering flocks were being monopolized by some shepherds who denied Jethro's daughters access to the troughs. Moses assisted the women by driving the shepherds away, so their flocks could be watered. Zipporah was among the sisters helped by Moses.

Zipporah and her sisters took Moses back to their tent to meet their father, who liked Moses. Moses stayed there in Midian, and later married Zipporah and began a new life. Zipporah gave birth to a son. Moses named him Gershom, a name that means "a foreigner there." Later, Zipporah had another son, Exodus 18:4.

Question: What is the name of Moses second son?

Answer in the back of book

The name Gershom is mentioned in Judges 18:30, it states that Jonathan was the descendant of Gershom who was the son of Moses, and his sons served as priests for the tribe of Dan until the time of the Babylon exile.

Gershom is the spelling of the eldest son of Levi in 1 Chronicles 6 and 1 Chronicles 15:7, KJV; but this name is spelled Gershon in NIV and NLT Bibles.

According to Ezra 8:2, the name Gershom is also the name of a descendant of Phinehas who journeys with Ezra from Babylon to Jerusalem in the reign of Artaxerxes around 536 BC.

Gershon

The name Gershon is mentioned in the Bible 18 times. Beginning in Genesis 46:11, Gershon was listed as one of the sons of Levi, along with Kohath and Merari. Their father, Levi lived to be 137 years old, and his sons' names are mentioned again in Exodus 6:16, Numbers 3:17, 1 Chronicles 6:1, and 1 Chronicles 23:6.

Gershon is the eldest son of Levi and the father of the Gershonites. The Gershonites were one of the four main divisions among the Levites in biblical times. The others were the Kohathites, Merarites, and Aaronids. The Kohathites had the care of the vessels and objects within the sanctuary. The Merarites were in charged with the transportation and supervision of the structural components of the tabernacle.

Exodus 6:17, Numbers 3:18, and Numbers 3:21, list the descendants of Gershon which included his sons, Libni and Shimei each of whom became the ancestor of a clan. The Gershonites camped west of the tabernacle in the wilderness, Numbers 3:23. The responsibilities of the sons of Gershon in the "tent of meeting" were the care of the tabernacle which included components such as the tent and its coverings, screens, doors, and hangings, under the supervision of Ithamar the son of Aaron, Numbers 3:25-26, Numbers 4:28.

Note of Interests: The phrase "tent of meeting" (NIV)/tabernacle of the congregation (KJV) is used in the Old Testament, especially in the book of Exodus, Leviticus, and Numbers. The "tent of meeting" was the place where God would meet His people, Israel. The phrase "tent of meeting" was used as another name for the "Tabernacle of Moses." It was considered the place of worship for the people of Israel during their 40-year wilderness journey after leaving Egypt until the Temple was built. It was approximately 300 years later, after Solomon built the first Temple in Jerusalem, that the "tent of meeting" was no longer used.

~~~~~~~~~~~~

According to Numbers 4:21-23, the Lord spoke to Moses telling him to count the sons of Gershon, throughout the house of their fathers, by families from the age of 30 years old up to 50 years old, to do the work in the "tent of meeting." The sons of Gershon numbered 2,630, Numbers 4:38-41.

Moses gave the sons of Gershon two wagons and four oxen, as their work required, Numbers 7:7. The sons of Merari were given four wagons and eight oxen, according to their work needs, but the sons of Kohath, Moses gave nothing. The Kohathites were to carry on their shoulders the holy things, like the utensils and symbols, for which they were responsible for, Numbers 7:9. The tabernacle was taken down by the sons of Gershon and Merari, Numbers 10:17.

According to Number 26, after the plague, the taking of the second census of Israel was command by the Lord to Moses and Eleazar, the priest. They were to number the Israelite families regarding those who were 20 years old or older and able to fight in the army of Israel. The total was 601,730 men. Then the Lord told Moses to divide the land among the tribal groups by their population, Numbers 26:51-56. The tribe of Levi reads as follow:

These were the Levites who were
counted by their clans:
Through Gershon, the Gershonite clan:
Through Kohath, the Kohathite clan;
Through Merari, the Merarite clan;
Numbers 26:57 NIV

Joshua the 21st chapter speaks of the 13 cities that were assigned to the Gershonites in northern Canaan by Eleazar and Joshua. According to Joshua 21:6, the clan of Gershon was allotted 13 cities from the tribes of Issachar, Asher, Naphtali, and the half-tribe of Manasseh in Bashan. The city Golan in Bashan was a city of refuge for an individual accused of murder, Joshua 21:27

Among the Gershonites who achieved distinction in later Biblical times was the family of Asaph. They were the singers from the time of David to the days of the Second Temple, 1 Chronicles 6:31-47, 1 Chronicles 25:1-7, Ezra 2:41, Nehemiah 12:35.

Beginning at 1 Chronicles 29:1, King David announced to the whole assembly that his son, Solomon is whom God has chosen to build the Temple. King David made every effort to obtain the materials for the Temple which included gold, silver, bronze, iron, timber, precious stones and gems, stones for mosaics, and large quantities of marble.

King David asked the leaders of the clans, the chiefs of the tribes, the army commanders, and the administrators of the royal property to volunteer to give to the building of the future Temple. Those who gave precious stones gave them to the Temple treasure, which was administered by Jehiel of the Levite clan of Gershon, 1 Chronicles 29:8.

According to 2 Chronicles 29, Hezekiah was 25 years old when he became king and reigned 29 years in Jerusalem. In the first month of his reign, he restored the temple worship, opened the doors of the temple and repaired them. King

Hezekiah then brought in priests and Levites to consecrate the temple of the Lord. They removed all the idols, altar groves and whatever that wasn't pleasing to the Lord, the God of their ancestors. The Gershonites, Joah the son of Zimmah and Eden the son of Joah are mentioned among those who purified and restored the temple of the Lord in the days of Hezekiah, 2 Chronicles 29:12.

Chapter 8

69

Gad

Who is Gad(s)? The name is mentioned 69 times in the Bible; 68 times in the Old Testament and once in the New Testament. Bible scholars believe there are at least two people in the Bible named Gad. One of the individuals was a personal prophet of King David of Israel, and the other Gad is one of the 12 sons of Jacob.

Beginning in Genesis 30, Rachel became jealous of her sister, Leah because she had children by Jacob. Rachel recognized that she was barren, so she gave her maidservant, Bilhah for Jacob to have sexual relations with so that she could have children through her. Bilhah became pregnant, and she had a son and named him Dan, and she became pregnant again, and he was named Naphtali.

When Leah stopped having children by Jacob, she gave her maidservant Zilpah to Jacob to have more children for her by him. When Leah's maidservant gave birth to a son, she named him Gad which means "How Fortunate!"

Note of Interests: Zilpah also had another son by Jacob named Asher, Genesis 35:26. Leah already had four sons by Jacob. The first son was named Reuben, and the second son was named Simeon, and the third son was named Levi, and the fourth son was named Judah, then she stopped having children, Genesis 29:31-35. However, sometimes later Leah became pregnant again and gave birth to Issachar, Zebulun, and a daughter named Dinah. Rachel eventually gave birth to Jacob last two sons, Joseph and Benjamin, whom she died while giving birth to, Genesis 35:18.

~~~~~~~~~~~~

Gad, the seventh son of Jacob, was the father of the tribe of Gad. They made the journey with Jacob from Paddan Aram to Canaan, and later, to Egypt, Genesis 46. Genesis 46:16, list Gad's sons who were Zephon, Haggi, Shuni, Ezbon, Eri, Arodi, and Areli.

In chapters 48 and 49 of Genesis, when Jacob was on his deathbed, he had his 12 sons to gather around him. He gave prophecies to his sons, telling them what will happen to them in the future. According to Genesis 49:19, he gave his son Gad the following prophecy:

Gad will be attacked by marauding bands,
but he will attack them when they retreat.
Genesis 49:19 NLT

Exodus 1, list the names of the sons of Israel who went to Egypt with Jacob, each with their own family. Gad name is mentioned in verse 4. Back in Genesis 45, Joseph makes himself known to his brothers who had sold him into slavery when he was 17-year-old. Approximately 22 years later, his brothers came to Egypt seeking grain because there was a famine in Canaan. They didn't recognize him, but he recognized them. At that time, Joseph had risen to power and was over the issuing of the grains. After Joseph made himself known to his brothers he asked Pharaoh could he move his family to Egypt, and he was granted permission.

The first chapter of Exodus list the 70 descendants of Jacob that lived in Egypt. Over time, they multiplied greatly, increased in numbers and the land was filled with them. Over the years, a new Pharaoh came into power in Egypt, and he feared the Israelites because they were numerous. So, he put slave master over them to oppress them with forced labor, and they built Pithom and Rameses as store cities for Pharaoh.

Next, the name "Gad" appears in the book of Numbers, chapter 1 where the first census of the people is recorded. The Israelites were oppressed in Egypt approximately 430 years. In Exodus 3, the Lord told Moses he had seen the misery of his people in Egypt and heard their cries. The Lord sent Moses to deliver the Israelites out of the hand of the Egyptians. After the deliverance, the Lord spoke to Moses in the wilderness of Sinai on the 1st day of the 2nd month of the 2nd year after the Israelites came out of Egypt. The Lord told Moses to take a census of the children of Israel, by their clans, and list every man by name, who was 20 years old or more. A man from each tribe was to assist Moses and Aaron with this census. Numbers 1:14, states from Gad's tribe, Eliasaph son of Deuel was chosen to help with the census.

Numbers 1:24- 25, states from the children of Gad there were 45,650 men, 20 years old or older.

Next, the name "Gad" appears in verse 14 of 2nd Numbers. It tells us that the tribe of Gad was camped next to Simeon tribe, and Eliasaph was the leader of the people of Gad. In Numbers 7, after Moses finished setting up the tabernacle, he anointed and consecrated it. The tribal leaders then made offerings to the Lord. On the sixth day Eliasaph, the leader of the people of Gad, brought his offering to the tabernacle.

In the book of Numbers 13, the Lord told Moses to send men to explore the land of Canaan; the Promise Land. A leader from each tribe was sent, and Geuel, son of Maki, was sent from the tribe of Gad, Number 13:15.

According to Numbers 26, the Lord instructed Moses to conduct a 2nd census, and the clans of Gad was numbered as 40,500, Numbers 26:15 & 18. The descendants of Gad by their clans were as follow:

1. Zephon, the Zephonite clan
2. Haggi, the and Haggite clan
3. Shuni, the Shunite clan
4. Ozni, the Oznite clan
5. Eri, the Erite clan
6. Arodi, the Arodite clan
7. Areli, the Arelite clan

According to Numbers 32:1, 2, the tribes settling east of the Jordan were Reuben and Gad. They had a great multitude of livestock. They spoke to Moses, Eleazar the priest, and to the leaders of the congregation asking for Ataroth, Dibon, Jazer, Nimrah, Heshbon, Elealeh, Shebam, Nebo, and Beon, the land which the Lord had subdued their enemies.

According to Numbers 32:25-32, the land that Reuben and Gad desired was to be granted to them on the condition that they would send their soldiers to help fight with their brethren in Canaan; the Promise Land. If they failed to perform their promise, those lands would be forfeited, and then they would have to come across the Jordan River and fight for a settlement like the rest of their brethren.

In the book of Deuteronomy, "Gad" is mentioned in chapters 27 and 33. According to Deuteronomy 27, curses and blessing were pronounced from Mount Ebal. After setting up the Law and renewing the covenant in Canaan, Israel was to proclaim upon the land the blessing, and the curse of the Law commanded in Deuteronomy 11:29. Six tribes were to stand on Mount Gerizim and six on Mount Ebal. The six tribes on Mount Gerizim was to announce the blessing, and the six tribes on Mount Ebal was to pronounce the curses of obeying the Law. The tribes who bless the people on Mount Gerizim were Simeon, Levi, Judah, Issachar, Joseph, and Benjamin. The tribes who stood on Mount Ebal and pronounce the curses were Reuben, Gad, Asher, Zebulun, Dan, and Naphtali, Deuteronomy 27:13.

Deuteronomy 33 gives, Moses' final blessing on Israel. To Gad, Moses said:

"Blessed is he who enlarges Gad's domain!
Gad lives there like a lion, tearing at arm or head.

**He chose the best land for himself; the
leader's portion was kept for him.
When the heads of the people assembled,
he carried out the Lord's righteous will,
and his judgments concerning Israel."**
Deuteronomy 33:20-21 NIV

According to Joshua 4:12, the men of Reuben, Gad, and half the tribe of Manasseh crossed over Jordan River armed before the children of Israel, as Moses had spoken to them. It was about 40,000 men prepared for war, who crossed over into the plains of Jericho. On that day the Lord exalted Joshua in the sight of all Israel.

The territory assigned to the tribe of Gad, and the children of Gad by Moses is given in details in Joshua 13:24-28. He gave them the territory of Jazer, and all the cities of Gilead, and half the land of the Ammonites, as far as Aroer near Rabbah. Gad's land included the area from Heshbon to Ramath Mizpah and Betonim, and from Mahanaim to the border of Debir. They were also given the Valley Beth Haram, Beth Nimrah, Succoth, and Zaphon, including the rest of the kingdom of King Sihon of Heshbon, along the Jordan River as its border, all the way up to the edge of the Sea of Galilee, on the other side of the Jordan River; eastward.

According to Joshua 18:7, the Levites received no territory inheritance. Gad, Reuben, and half the tribe of Manasseh had received their inheritance beyond the Jordan River on the east. The descendants of Gad dwelt next to the Reubenites, and they lived in the land of Bashan as far east as Salekah, 1 Chronicles 5:11.

In 1 Chronicles 6:63 and Joshua 21:7, it states that the descendants of Merari received by sacred lots, 12 towns from the territories of Reuben, Gad, and Zebulun. The sons of Levi were Gershon, Kohath, and Merari. The Levites were allotted no territorial inheritance of their own at the "Division of The Promised Land." God was their inheritance, Numbers 18:20 and Deuteronomy 10:9.

Joshua the 20th chapter speaks of the cities of refuge. The Lord spoke to Joshua, telling him to have the Israelites to designate cities of refuge. They were for anyone who kills a person unintentionally could flee there and find protection from the avenger of blood. The individual could flee to one of these cities and stand at the entrance of the city gate. He would state his case before the elders of that city. Then the elders would admit the fugitive into their city and provide a place for that person to live among them. If the avenger of blood pursues him, they won't give the manslayer into his hands. He would stay in the city until his case is decided by the assembly and he must continue to live in that city until the high priest who was in office at the time of the incident. Then the one who committed manslaughter may return home to the city from which he fled, Joshua 20:1-5. According to Joshua 20:8, from the tribe of Gad, the city of Ramoth in Gilead was set aside for the city of refuge.

According to Joshua 22, after Israel had fought their enemies, the men of the Eastern Tribes which were Reuben, Gad and East Manasseh were allowed to return home, departing from the people of Israel at Shiloh, Joshua 22:1-9. The Eastern Tribes (Reuben, Gad and the half-tribe of

Manasseh) built an altar by Jordan. When Israel heard about it they assembly the people to gather at Shiloh to make war against them because they thought they were turning away from the Lord. The people of Reuben, the people of Gad and the half-tribe of Manasseh, explained that the altar wasn't for burnt, grain or peace offerings. The children of Reuben and the children of Gad called the altar, Witness, "For it is a witness between us that the Lord is God."

First Chronicles 12:8-14 speak of the sons of Gad, who were warriors who joined David at Ziklag when he was a fugitive running from Saul. They were fierce as lions and quick as gazelles. They were prepared to fight with shields and spears. There were a total of 11 men, and they were all army commanders.

In the book of Ezekiel 48, Gad is mentioned three times. In the division of the land, Ezekiel 48:27, says by the border of Zebulun's land, from the east to the west side, Gad shall have one portion. Then verse 28, speaks of the southern boundary of Gad which runs from Tamar to the waters of Meribah Kadesh and then follows the Brook of Egypt toward the Mediterranean Sea.

Further in this chapter, Gad's name is mentioned in the gates of the new city. Verse 34, says the gates of the new city were named after the tribes of Israel. The three gates on the west wall, which was about 1 ½ miles long, were named Gad, Asher, and Naphtali. Ezekiel 48:35, tells us that the distance around the entire city would be 6 miles, and the name of the city will be called "The Lord Is There."

The name "Gad" is mentioned in 1 Samuel 13:7. When the Israelite army realized that they were outnumbered and losing the battle with the Philistines, some of them hid in caves, bushes, and in tombs. Others hid in deep dry pits, while others crossed on the other side of the Jordan River and went to Gad and Gilead. Saul's stayed at Gilgal where the prophet Samuel arrived and told Saul, he offered an unlawful sacrifice to the Lord, 1 Samuel 13:1-16.

The Prophet Gad

The other Gad mentioned in the Bible is a prophet. His first appearance is in 1 Samuel 22:5. The prophet Gad is persuading David to leave his place of safety in Moab and return to the forest of Hereth in the land of Judah where the jealous King Saul awaited him. Gad is described as David's seer in 1 Chronicles 21:9.

The next biblical reference to the prophet Gad is 2 Samuel 24. The Lord told Gad to give David three choices, and one of those would be his punishment for taking a census which the Lord didn't instruct David to do. The three choices were as follow:

1. 3 years of famine
2. 3 months of destruction by the sword of your enemies,
3. 3 days of severe plague as the angel of the Lord brings devastation throughout the land of Israel

David chose the three-day plague for his punishment. During the plague, the Lord took 70,000 lives. The prophet Gad then told David to build an altar to the Lord on the threshing floor of Araunah, the Jebusite, 2 Samuel 24:18. The burnt offerings on the altar would cause the Lord to stop the plague. This threshing floor became the site of King Solomon Temple. This biblical event is also mentioned in 1 Chronicles 21.

According to 2 Chronicles 29:25, King Hezekiah had the Levites to stand in the Temple of the Lord with cymbals, harps and lyres in the way prescribed by David, Gad the king's seer and Nathan the prophet which was commanded by the Lord through his prophets.

According to 1 Chronicles 29:29, all the events of King David's reign, from beginning to end are written in the chronicles of Samuel the Seer, in the chronicles of Nathan the prophet, and the chronicles of Gad the Seer. These chronicles included the mighty deeds of David's reign. It describes everything that happened to David, and to Israel and to all the surrounding kingdoms.

A Palestinian city named Halhul has a tomb attributed to Gad.

The name "Gad" is mentioned in the book of Jeremiah 49, in a message concerning the Ammonites. It reads:

This message was given concerning the Ammonites.
This is what the Lord says:
"Are there no descendants of Israel
to inherit the land of Gad?
Why are you, who worship Molech,
living in its towns?"
Jeremiah 49:1 NLT

The name "Gad" is mentioned once in King James Bible, New Testament. In the book of Revelation, chapter 7, Gad is among the tribes who are promised the Seal of God for 12,000 of its members. According to Revelation 7:4-5, John heard the number of those who were sealed.

Then I heard the number of those who were sealed:
144,000 from all the tribes of Israel.
From the tribe of Judah 12,000 were sealed,
from the tribe of Reuben 12,000,
from the tribe of Gad, 12,000,
Revelation 7:4-5 NIV

Chapter 9

GEDALIAH
AND GEHAZI

Gedaliah "Ged-a-li-ah"

Five men in the Bible are named Gedaliah. They are all mentioned in the Old Testament. The name is pronounced "ged-l-ahy-uh." The name means "God is my greatness," and it is written 31 times in the KJV Bible. The most well-known man of these five is the Jewish leader whom King Nebuchadnezzar assigned to serve as governor of Judah after the destruction of the temple, 2 Kings 25:22-26.

It was during the time of the Babylonian siege when Nebuchadnezzar defeated Jerusalem and looted and destroyed the temple in 587 BC. Judah's King Zedekiah and most of the Jews who survived were taken into exile to Babylon. The Babylonian soldiers are also referred to as Chaldeans. They pulled the walls down, burned the builds, and leveled Jerusalem to the ground.

After the destruction of the temple, Nebuchadnezzar departed from Judea, leaving Gedaliah, with Chaldean soldiers, at Mizpah to govern the vinedressers and husbandmen who were exempted from captivity, Jeremiah 40:5 and Jeremiah 52:16.

Only the most destitute Jews were left behind in Judah to grow crops and tend the land. The Babylon King, Nebuchadnezzar appointed Gedaliah to serve as his Jewish governor over the region, and he served as governor from the town of Mizpah, north of Jerusalem. It was typical for a conquered people to be given a governor from among their own people to serve as a representative between Babylon and his fellow kinsmen. Chaldean soldiers remained in the land to keep order and make sure no rebellion took place.

When those who had fled from Babylon's invasion heard that Gedaliah had been established as governor, they returned to Judah. Among those who returned were several groups of soldiers who had not been in Jerusalem during the siege. As they arrived, Gedaliah urged everyone to accept their fate and live at peace in the land under the rule of the Babylonians, and they would have nothing to fear. The Chaldeans would not harm them if they remained peaceful.

"Settle down in the land and serve the king of Babylon, and it will go well with you."
2 Kings 25:24 NIV

The prophet Jeremiah jointed Gedaliah, and the city of Mizpah became the popular location for Jews from various cities and towns, Jeremiah 40:6, 11. Judah enjoyed peace, prosperity, and harvested an abundance of wine and summer fruit, Jeremiah 40:12. However, this peace didn't last long.

Gedaliah was told about a plot to kill him by Johanan who was one of the captains that had escaped the Babylonian exile. Another captain named Ishmael was working in league with the king of the Ammonites to kill Gedaliah. Johanan request permission to execute Ishmael quietly to preserve Gedaliah's life and maintain the peace in the land. Gedaliah, however, refused to believe that Ishmael would actually kill him.

The king of Ammon wanted Gedaliah dead because the Ammonites had been allies with the previous king of Judah against the Babylonians. Now, Gedaliah was cooperating with the Babylonians. The king of Ammon also believed, if the Babylonians were forced to deal with a new rebellion in Judah, it would delay their impending attacks against Ammonites. In any case, Ishmael had indeed been sent to betray and kill Gedaliah.

Gedaliah was convinced of Ishmael's loyalty that he welcomed Ishmael, and ten men to sit and eat with him, Jeremiah 41:1. Ishmael and his men killed Gedaliah and those who were with him, including the Chaldean soldiers. Gedaliah had only been the governor for two months.

The following day, Ishmael slaughtered 70 pilgrims from the north who had come to worship at the temple. Finally, Ishmael took captive everyone in Mizpah and headed toward Ammon. Before he could get away, Johanan, the one who had warned Gedaliah about the plot, chased Ishmael down and rescued the captives. Ishmael escaped with eight of his men and returned to the Ammonites.

The Jewish leaders established in memory of Gedaliah's tragic death, a fast. The Fast of Gedaliah which falls every year on the 3rd day of the Hebrew month of Tishrei, and it is still recognized in Judaism.

The other four men named Gedaliah are as follows:

1. One of the six sons of Jeduthun was named Gedaliah. He served as a musician during the reign of King David for the ministry of prophesying, accompanied by harps, lyres, and cymbals, 1 Chronicles 25:1-9.
2. The grandfather of the prophet Zephaniah and father of Cushi was named Gedaliah, Zephaniah 1:1.
3. 3According to Ezra 10:18, a descendant of the priests had broken God's Law by marrying foreign women during the time of Ezra was named Gedaliah.
4. One of King Zedekiah's men who helped cast the prophet Jeremiah into a muddy well was named Gedaliah. They wanted to keep Jeremiah from telling the people that all who stayed in Jerusalem during the Babylonian siege would die, but those who left the city and surrendered would live, Jeremiah 38:1-6.

Gehazi   "gee-HAY-zai"

Gehazi is an individual mentioned in the 2nd book of Kings who was a servant of Elisha, the prophet. Gehazi was in a position of power, but he was corrupt and misused his authority. As a punishment, Elisha cursed him, transferring Naaman's leprosy to him and his descendants forever.

Gehazi named is mentioned first in 2 Kings 4 in the history of the Shunammite woman and her son. This biblical event involved four individuals: Elisha who is God's prophet, Gehazi his servant, the wealthy and religious Shunammite woman, and her young son, who was born miraculously. The event takes place in the territory of Issachar in northern Israel during the reign of Jehoram (Joram), the second son of Ahab and Jezebel around 850 BC.

The Shunammite woman had set aside a living quarter for Elisha in her home whenever he came to Shunem, 2 Kings 4:9-10. Her son is born because of a miracle spoke by Elisha, 2 Kings 4:14-17. Years later, when her son dies, she takes his body to Elisha's room in her house, lay him on Elisha's bed, and shuts the door behind her. She and her servants travel about 15 miles to see Elisha on a donkey at Mount Carmel, 2 Kings 4:21-25.

Elisha notices her approaching and asks Gehazi, his servant to run and meet her and inquire after her well-being. She told Gehazi that everything was well, but when she came to the man of God, she fell to the ground before him and caught hold of his feet. Elisha told Gehazi to travel back to her home, and take his staff, and lay it on the child's face. The woman refuses to return home unless Elisha went with her.

Gehazi laid the staff on the child's face, and there was no life. Gehazi met Elisha and told him the child was indeed dead. Elisha then went in alone and shut the door behind him and prayed to the Lord. He then laid down on the child's body, placing his mouth on the child's mouth, his eyes on the child's eyes, and his hands on the child's hands. As Elisha stretched over the child's body, his body began to grow warm, again. Elisha summoned Gehazi and told him to call the child's mother. She took her son in her arms and carried him downstairs. She was overwhelmed with gratitude, 2 Kings 4:29-37.

Another well-known biblical event that involved Gehazi is recorded in 2 Kings 5. Naaman was a mighty fierce warrior for the king of Aram, even though he suffered from leprosy. A young girl was captured during his Aramean raids and given to his wife as a maid. One day the girl told her mistress that she wished her master would go visit a prophet in Samaria and he would heal him of his leprosy.

Naaman told the Aram king what the young girl from Israel said, and the king told Naaman to go. The king gave Naaman an introduction letter to take to the king of Israel. The king also sent with Naaman gifts, 750 pounds of silver, 150 pounds of gold and 10 sets of clothing. When the king of Israel read the letter, he tore his clothes in dismay. He then said, "Am I God, that I can give life and take it away? Why is this man asking me to heal someone with leprosy? I can see that he's just trying to pick a fight with me."

When Elisha heard what the king of Israel had done, he sent the king a message telling him to send Naaman to him so Naaman can learn that there is a real prophet here in Israel. So Naaman arrived at the door of Elisha's house with his chariots, but Elisha sent a messenger out to him. He told Naaman to go and wash 7 times in the Jordan River, and then he would be healed. Naaman became angry and stalked away. He thought the prophet would have come out to meet him, wave his hand over him, and call on the name of his God and then he would be healed of leprosy.

Naaman didn't want to wash in Jordan River because it wasn't clean as Damascus, the Abana, and the Pharpar. His officers encouraged Naaman to go and wash in the Jordan River. When he did, his skin became healthy as the skin of a young child.

Naaman and his entire party went back to find the man of God to give him gifts. Elisha refused to accept the gifts from Naaman. Gehazi, the servant of Elisha, thought to himself that his master shouldn't have let this Aramean get away without taking any of his gifts. So, he set off after Naaman, and when Naaman saw him, he climbed down from his chariot and met him. Gehazi said his master has sent him because two young prophets from the hill country of Ephraim have just arrived, and he would like 75 pounds of silver and two sets of clothing to give them.

Gehazi took the gifts and hid them inside the house.

When Elisha asked Gehazi where he been, he stated nowhere. Elisha told Gehazi he was there in spirit when Naaman stepped down from his chariot to meet him, and since he had done this, he and his descendants will suffer from Naaman's leprosy forever. Gehazi left the room covered with leprosy, and his skin was white as snow.

Gehazi is also mentioned in 2 Kings 8, twice. He is telling the king about the biblical events in 2 Kings 4, as the Shunammite woman appears before the king with her son that was restored to life concerning her house and her land, 2 Kings 8:4,5.

Chapter 10

THE MIGHTY WARRIOR

Gideon

The King James Bible only mentioned one man named Gideon out of the 66 books of the Bible. His name means "he who cuts down." He is also known by the names, Jerubbaal and Jerubbesheth. Gideon was an Israel judge, prophet and a military leader who won a battle through faith rather than the strength of his army. His acts and deeds are only mentioned in the book of Judges, chapters 6, 7, and 8.

Beginning in Judges 6, the angel of the Lord came and sat down under the oak tree in Ophrah. This oak tree belonged to Joash the Abiezrite, where his son Gideon was threshing wheat in a winepress to hide the grain from the Midianites, Judges 6:11. Ophrah was a small city in Manasseh, but the exact location is uncertain. It is mentioned in relations to the Jezreel Valley and Mount Tabor where Joash sons were put to death on Mount Tabor by the Midianites. His only remaining son was Gideon.

Gideon's father, Joash is a descendant of Abiezer, the head of one of the families of the tribe of Manasseh that settled west of the Jordan, Joshua 17:1-6. Gideon's name means "cutter down." He was responsible for tearing down his father's altar to Baal and cutting down the Asherah Pole. This was Gideon first act of obedience to the Lord, Judges 6:26. Afterward, Gideon was called Jerubbaal which means "Let Baal defend himself."

In Judges 6, we find Gideon threshing wheat in a winepress, of all places, and it was probably in June. Usually, threshing wheat was done in an open, breezy area; like a hilltop to aid in winnowing the threshed grain.

Note of Interests: A winepress in Biblical times consisted of a square or circular pit cut out of rocks, and it would be lined with stones and sealed with plaster. In the pit, grapes would be dumped into the upper winepress where they would be crushed under bare feet. The juice would then flow through a conduit into a lower vessel, the wine vat. The fact that Gideon was threshing grain in a confined winepress shows his fear of being seen by the Midianites, who would take the grains.

~~~~~~~~~~~

When the angel of the Lord appeared to Gideon, he said, "The Lord is with you, mighty warrior," Judges 6:12. Gideon replied, "but if the Lord is with us, why has all this happened to us? Where are all his wonders that our ancestor told us about? How the Lord brought us up out of Egypt? But now the Lord has abandoned us and put us into the hand of Midian," Judges 6:13.

Note of Interests: The angel of the Lord finds Gideon threshing in a winepress because of fear. It is ironic that the angel calls Gideon "mighty warrior" (NIV, NRSV) or "mighty man of valor" (KJV). This is a Hebrew phrase "gibbor hayil" used to describe David's select warriors who had performed heroic acts while fighting with David in battles. God sees and recognizes something in Gideon that he doesn't recognize in himself; a mighty warrior.

~~~~~~~~~~~~

The Lord turned to Gideon and said, "Go in the strength you have and rescue Israel from the Midianites. Am I not sending you?" Gideon replied, "but Lord how can I save Israel? My clan is the weakest and smallest in the tribe of Manasseh, and I am the least in my entire family." The Lord answered, "I will be with you, and you will strike down all the Midianites together," Judges 6:14-16.

Note of Interests: Gideon proclaims his weaknesses, like Moses, when God called him, Exodus 3:11, Exodus 4:10-12. God gave Gideon the same answer he gave Moses, "I will be with you."

~~~~~~~~~~~~

The Lord makes a great promise to Gideon. He told Gideon, he will strike down all the Midianites together, in one mighty battle, not just one at a time, Judges 6:16.

Gideon replied, "If I have found favor in your eyes, give me a sign that it is indeed you speaking to me. Please do not go until I come back and bring my offering and set it before you." And the Lord said, "I will wait until you return."

Gideon prepared a young goat and made bread without yeast. He put the meat in a basket, the broth in a pot, and offered them to him under the oak tree. The angel of God said to Gideon, "take the meat and the unleavened bread, and place them on a rock." The angel of the Lord touched the meat and the unleavened bread with the tip of the staff which was in his hand. Suddenly, a fire blazed from the rock, consuming the meat and the bread, and the angel of the Lord disappeared, Judges 6:17-21.

Note of Interests: Like Gideon, Abraham prepared a meal for his three guests in the same manner. He also asked the angels of the Lord to wait while he made the meal for them, Genesis 18. Gideon prepared a young goat with unleavened bread, and Abraham prepared a young calf with unleavened bread. A little further in the same chapter, the Lord told Abraham that Sarah would bear a son, by this time next year, verse 10.

~~~~~~~~~~

When Gideon saw the meal consumed by fire, he was frightened, but the Lord said to him, "Peace! Do not be afraid. You are not going to die." At this site, Gideon built an altar to the Lord, and named it "The Lord is Peace." This altar still stands in the town of Ophrah of the Abiezrites, Judges 6:22-24.

Note of Interests: Gideon's ancestors, Abram (Abraham), Isaac, and Jacob, also built altars to commemorate the appearance of the Lord, Genesis 12:7, Genesis 13:18, Genesis 26:25, and Genesis 28:18.

~~~~~~~~~~~

On the same night, the Lord commanded Gideon to destroy his father's altar that was built for Baal, and make an altar for the Lord, then sacrifice a young bull on it. Gideon was fearful of his relatives, so he took ten men in the middle of the night and did what the Lord commanded, Judges 6:25-27.

The men of the city arose in the morning and saw that the altar of Baal was torn down along with the Asherah pole. They noticed that a bull had been offered on the altar which had been built. When the men found out that Gideon had torn down the altar they told his father to bring him to them, so they could kill him. Joash, Gideon's father, refused, he said to the men "let Baal contend for himself if he is a god." On that day Gideon was called "Jerubbaal," which means "Let Baal defend himself" because he had broken down Baal's altar," Judges 6:32.

According to Judges 6:33, the Midianites, Amalekites and other eastern people joined forces and crossed over the Jordan River and camped in the Valley of Jezreel. The "Spirit of the Lord" came upon Gideon which gave him courage and power. He blew a trumpet to summon Abiezer's family to follow him. Then Gideon sent messengers throughout

Manasseh, Asher, Zebulun, and Naphtali to gather their warriors.

Afterward, Gideon asked God for a sign if he would save Israel by his hands as he had promised. Gideon told God he would place a wool fleece on the threshing floor, and if morning dew was only on the fleece and all the ground was dry, then he would know for sure that Israel would be delivered by his hands. When Gideon awoke the next morning, it was so. He squeezed from the fleece a bowl full of water and the ground was dry.

According to Judges 6:38, Gideon asked God not to let his anger burn against him because he wants to make another request. He asked God to allow the fleece to remain dry, while the ground around it is wet with dew. God did as Gideon requested.

Note of Interests: Gideon lacked strength, courage, and faith. There was no way Gideon was going into battle without some proof that the Lord would be with him. Gideon witnessed the following signs from the Lord.

1. The consuming of the meat and the unleavened bread by fire.
2. The dry fleece on the wet threshing floor.
3. The wet fleece on the dry threshing floor.

The Lord was patient with Gideon. He gave him all the signs he needed to increase his faith. The only other time God was so patient with someone persistently asking for signs was in Moses case. In both cases, the Lord was planning the deliverance of his people using these two men. The Lord told Moses, he was sending him to deliver his people out of Egypt. Listed below are the three signs God gave Moses to increase his faith, Exodus 4:3-9.

1. The Lord told Moses to throw his staff on the ground, and it became a serpent, and Moses ran from it. The Lord then told Moses to put forth his hand, and take it by the tail, and it became a staff again.
2. The Lord told Moses to put his hand in his bosom, and it came out full of leprosy when Moses obediently repeated the process, his hand was completely restored.
3. The Lord asked Moses to take water from the Nile and pour it on the dry ground, and the water turned into blood.

~~~~~~~~~~~~

In chapter 7 of Judges, Gideon and his men camped at the spring of Harod, while the army of the Midianites camped north of them in the valley near the hill of Moreh. The Lord told Gideon, he had too many men for him to give him victory over the Midianites, for Israel would become boastful, believing their own power has delivered them from the Midianites.

The Lord told Gideon, the men who were fearful could leave and go home. So, 22,000 of them left, and 10,000 men were willing to fight, Judges 7:3. The Lord told Gideon, he still had too many men. Next, the Lord told Gideon, to take the men down to the water and separate every man who laps the water with his tongue, as a dog laps, from those who kneel and drunk with their mouths in the stream. Three hundred men out of the 10,000 men drank from cupped hands, lapping like dogs. All the rest got down on their knees to drink. The Lord told Gideon, he would deliver the Midianites into his hands with the 300 men who lapped and let all the other men go to his home. Gideon sent the other men of Israel home, but the 300 men who stayed kept all the supplies and rams' horns.

The camp of Midian was located below Gideon in the valley. Now, the same night the Lord told Gideon to arise and go down to their camp for he will give it into Israel's hand. The Lord told Gideon to take his servant Purah with him if he was afraid. So, they went down to the outposts of the enemy army camp, Judges 7:10. The Lord told Gideon he would hear what the Midianites were saying and afterward he would be greatly encouraged.

Now the Midianites, Amalekites, and all the sons of the east were lying in the valley as numerous as locusts, and their camels were too many to count. Gideon crept up just as a man was telling his friend about a dream. The man dream that a cake of barley bread came tumbling down into the Midianites camp, and it hit a tent, turned it over, and the tent was knocked down flat! The man's friend replied, "This is nothing less than the sword of Gideon the son of Joash, a man of Israel; God has given Midian and all the camp into Gideon's hand."

After Gideon heard the dream and its interpretation, he bowed in worship before the Lord. Gideon returned to the camp of Israel and said, "Arise, the Lord has given the camp of Midian into your hands," Judge 7:15. Gideon divided 300 men into three groups. Each man was given a trumpet and a clay jar with a torch in it. Gideon told the men to do as he does when they get to the edge of the enemy camp. It was around midnight when Gideon and the 100 men with him reached the edge of the Midianite camp. Suddenly, they blew their trumpets and broke their clay jars. The torches were held in their left hands and the trumpets in their right hands for blowing. The men cried, "A sword for the Lord and for Gideon!" When the 300 Israelites blew their trumpets, the Lord caused the warriors in the enemy camp to fight each other with their swords.

Note of Interests: Gideon's victory over the Midianites with just 300 men and no weapons is considered unbelievable, impossible; a miracle. But that is how God wanted to give Israel the victory, so they would remember this phenomenon battle for generations to come.

KJV   Not by might, nor by power, but by my spirit, saith the Lord of hosts. Zechariah 4:6

NIV   Not by might nor by power, but by my Spirit, says the Lord Almighty. Zechariah 4:6

NLT   It is not by force nor by strength, but by my Spirit, says the Lord of Heaven's Armies. Zechariah 4:6

~~~~~~~~~~~~~

The Midianites who weren't killed fled to places as far as Beth-shittah near Zererah and to the border of Abel-meholah near Tabbath. Israel warriors captured the two leaders of Midian; Oreb and Zeeb. They killed Oreb at the rock of Oreb and Zeeb was killed at the winepress of Zeeb. The heads of Oreb and Zeeb were brought to Gideon from across the Jordan.

Gideon and his 300 men crossed the Jordan River pursuing Zebah and Zalmunna; the kings of Midian. When Gideon and his army reach Succoth, they asked the leaders of the town for food, and they refused them, Judges 8:5. Gideon told them after he had captured Zebah and Zalmunna he would return and tear their flesh with the thorns and briers from the wilderness. When Gideon and his army reached Penuel and asked for food for the army, they gave him a similar answer as the Succoth. Gideon told them when he returns safely, he would tear down their tower.

Gideon ambushed the armies of Zebah and Zalmunna while they weren't suspecting it. The two kings of Midian fled, Zebah and Zalmunna, and Gideon chased them down. When Gideon was returning from the battle by the Ascent of Heres, he captured a youth from Succoth and questioned him concerning the princes of Succoth and its elders. The youth wrote down the names of 77 men.

Gideon returned to Succoth and reminded them of how they taunted him concerning Zebah and Zalmunna. They wouldn't give his army bread to eat when they were weary and exhausted. Gideon took the elders of the city Succoth and disciplined them with thorns and briers from the wilderness. Next, Gideon tore down the tower of Penuel and killed the men of the city.

Gideon asked, "Zebah and Zalmunna what type of men did they killed at Tabor?" They answered, "they resembled the son of a king." Gideon replied, "They were his brothers, and if their lives had been spared, he wouldn't kill them." Gideon then told his first-born son named Jether to "rise and kill them," but he did not draw his sword because he was afraid, he was just a youngster, Judges 8:20.

According to Judges 8:21, Zebah and Zalmunna said to Gideon, "to rise up yourself, and fall on us." So, Gideon killed them both and took the crescent ornaments off their camel's necks. The people of Israel asked Gideon and his sons to rule over them because he had rescued them from the Midianites. But Gideon replied, "I will not rule over you, nor will my son. The Lord will rule over you," Judges 8:23.

Gideon requested that everyone give him a gold earring from the plunder that they collected from their fallen enemies. The Midianites were accustomed to wear gold earrings because they were Ishmaelites.

Note of Interests: According to the Book of Genesis, the Ishmaelites are the descendants of Ishmael. The older son of Abraham was by his wife Sarah's Egyptian slave, named Hagar. When Sarah couldn't conceive she gave her slave, Hagar, in marriage to Abraham, Genesis 16:3. Ishmael had twelve sons: Nabaioth, Kedar, Abdeel, Mabsam, Idumas, Masmoas, Massaos, Chodad, Theman, Jetur, Naphesus, and

Cadmas. They inhabited all the land from the Euphrates to the Red Sea, along with other territories.

~~~~~~~~~~~~

The men gladly spread out a garment and cast an earring of his prey into it. The weight of the gold earrings was 1,7000 shekels of gold which is about 43 pounds. This was in addition to the royal ornaments and pendants, the purple raiment worn by the kings of Midian, and the golden chains around the necks of their camels.

Gideon turned the gold into an ephod, and place it in his town, Ophrah. All Israel prostituted themselves by worshiping, and it became a snare to Gideon, and to his house.

Midian was crushed by the children of Israel, and the land had peace for 40 years.

According to Judges 8:30, Gideon had 70 sons, for he had many wives. He had another son by a concubine in Shechem who named was Abimelech. Gideon died at a ripe old age, and he was buried in the tomb of his father, Joash located in Ophrah of the Abiezrites.

As soon as Gideon died, the children of Israel turned again and prostituted themselves by worshiping the images of Baal, and made Baal-Berith their god.

The children of Israel forgot about the Lord their God, who had delivered them from their enemies on every side. They failed to show any loyalty to the family of Gideon and forgot the heroic deeds he had done for them, Judges 8:35.

Note of Interests: Even though Gideon name is mentioned 37 times in the KJV, his other name "Jerrubbaal" is mentioned 13 times in the book of Judges and once in 1 Samuel 12. It reads, "And the Lord sent Jerubbaal, Bedan, Jephthah, and Samuel, and delivered you out of the hand of your enemies on every side, and ye dwelled safe," 1 Samuel 12:11, KJV. Gideon is also called "Jerubbesheth" and is mentioned once in the KJV, 2 Samuel 11:21. It's about his son Abimelech who was killed by a woman at Thebez. She threw a millstone down on him from the city wall.

~~~~~~~~~~~~

Chapter 11

NEW
TESTAMENT
ONLY

Can you recall, the two "G – Men" whose names only appear in the New Testament? A brief description of each man is given, and hopefully, that will help.

Think . . . smile . . .

The answer can be found in Chapter 1

1. _____

This individual is mentioned 5 times, and his name is the name of several men in the New Testament. These "G – Men" were involved in the ministry of the apostles in one way or another. Paul baptized a man with this name. Paul also had a friend with this name that lived in Macedonia and Derbe. Another individual with this name was the friend of John who was commended for his hospitality toward traveling preachers of the gospel, his faithfulness, and his love for with the Lord.

2. _____

This individual name is mentioned 3 times only in the book of Acts also called "Acts of the Apostles." He was the Roman proconsul of Achaia under emperor Claudius when Paul visited Corinth around 53 AD, Acts 18:12. When the Jews made an insurrection against Paul and brought him before the judgment seat, this G-man refused to listen to the clamorous mob. He also refused to entertain their unjust demands. He had the Jews ejected from the court, and Paul was set free.

Chapter 12

A SPECIFIC
BIBLE BOOK

The "G – Men" names listed below only appears in one specific book of the Bible, at least twice. There are 66 books in the Bible, 39 are in Old Testament, and 27 are in the New Testament. The "G – Men" listed below have been discussed in the previous chapters, you have read.

Let's name the book of the Bible that their names can be found in. A little help has been provided. . . . *Don't forget to smile*

The answer can be found in Chapter 1

N_____	Gideoni (5)	Chapter 4
_____	Gideon (37)	Chapter 10
J_____	Gaal (9)	Chapter 6
1st K_____	Geber (2)	Chapter 3
_____	Ginath (2)	Chapter 3
_____	Gehazi (12)	Chapter 9
2nd _____	Gadi (2)	Chapter 3

Vanessa Rayner

1ˢᵗ C_____ Giddalti (2)   Chapter 3

1ˢᵗ C_____ Gazez (2)   Chapter 3

N_____ Ginnetho or Ginnethon (3) Chapter 3

J_____Gemariah (5)   Chapter 4

<u>A</u>_____ Gallio (3)   Chapter 3

P.S.:   Why don't you re-read the chapter(s) of the name(s) that you struggle with?

"In Jesus Name"

Chapter 13

ONE CHAPTER

This chapter contains the "G – Men" whose names only appear in **one chapter** of a **particular book** of the Bible. They have been discussed in the previous chapters, you have read.

Question: Which one can you say, a word or two about? Do you remember which G-man is only mentioned in the New Testament?

1. Gaal (9)   Judges 9:26   Judges 9:28   Judges 9:30
   Judges 9:31   Judges 9:35   Judges 9:36
   Judges 9:37   Judges 9:39   Judges 9:41

_____

_____

2. Gabbai (1)   Nehemiah 11:8

_____

_____

4. Gaddi (1)   Numbers 13:11

_____

_____

5. Gaddiel (1)   Numbers 13:10

_____

_____

6. Gadi (2)   2 Kings 15:14   2 Kings 15:17

_____

_____

7. Gaham (1)   Genesis 22:24

_____

_____

11. Gallio (3)   Acts 18:12   Acts 18:14   Acts 18:17

_____

_____

13. Gamul (1)   1 Chronicles 24:17

_____

_____

19. Geber (2)   1 Kings 4:13   1 Kings 4:19

_____

_____

23. Gemalli (1)   Numbers 13:12

_____

_____

25. Genubath (1)   1 Kings 11:20

_____

_____

29. Gesham or Geshan (1)   1 Chronicles 2:47

_____

_____

31. Geuel (1)   Numbers 13:15

_____

_____

32. Gibbar (1)   Ezra 2:20

_____

_____

33. Gibea (1)   1 Chronicles 2:49

_____

_____

34. Giddalti (2)   1 Chronicles 25:4   1 Chronicles 25:29

_____

_____

38. Gilalai (1)   Nehemiah 12:36

_____

_____

39. Ginath (2)   1 Kings 16:21   1 Kings 16:22

_____

_____

41. Gispa   or Gishpa (1)   Nehemiah 11:21

_____

_____

The "G – Men" you couldn't say a word or two about, take time and read those Bible chapters in its entirety. The biblical information leaving to their names will help you, at least recognize the individual name that is written in "The Word of God." *Hallelujah!*

Confession: I had to read every Chapter, except Acts 18 (Gallio). I have researched, read, re-read, and typed about them all, but I could on speak on 1, at this moment; (03/10/18 @ 1049). *Let's smile . . .*

Father God, I Love You, in spite of . . .

The chapters are listed below for your convenience. A few of these "G – Men" are mentioned in the same chapter.

_____   Judges 9

_____   Nehemiah 11

_____   Numbers 13

_____   2 Kings 15

_____   Genesis 22

_____   Acts 18

_____   1 Chronicles 24

_____   1 Kings 4

_____   1 Kings 11

_____   1 Chronicles 2

_____   Ezra 2

_____   1 Chronicles 25

_____   Nehemiah 12

_____   1 Kings 16

A Reader's Question

This new section just dropped in my spirit at 0613 on January 14, 2017, titled A Reader's Question.

An individual asked me the following question: "Have I thought about advertising my books by radio or doing monthly book signing?

<u>The Answer</u>:

I thought about it several times and prayed about it on numerous occasions; but Father God keep saying, "keep on reading, researching, studying, writing and typing."

Author's Closing Remarks

In closing, I am surprised!

When given this assignment by Father God, I was shocked by all the men's names that begin with the letter "G" in the Bible. I thought I would be working on this book to the end of 2018 but look at God! I just prayed and started working on one G name at a time and kept praying and asking for strength. I thought this book would have been at least 3 or 4 times bigger than this, but it's not.

One thing, I learned for sure while writing this book, if we, humans allow our carnal nature to look at, evaluate or even dwell on an assignment from Our Father, we'll talk ourselves out of a blessing! Praise God!

Pray for the Ministry . . . May the "LORD of Peace," give you His Peace.

Dr. Vanessa

References

Chapter 1   The List

1.   BibleGateway: https://www.biblegateway.com

Chapter 2   Only Once

1.   BibleGateway: https://www.biblegateway.com

Chapter 3   Two or Three Times

1.   Jacksonville Theological Seminary, Gallio
2.   Bible Study Tools: https://biblestudytools.com/dictionary

Chapter 4   Four or Five Times

1.   Wikipedia, The Free Encyclopedia: https://en.wikipedia.org/wiki
2.   BibleHub: https://biblehub.com

Chapter 5   Six or Seven Times

1.   Wikipedia, The Free Encylopedia: https://en.wikipedia.org/wiki
2.   BibleGateway: https://www.biblegateway.com

Chapter 6   Gaal and Gera

1.   Wikipedia, The Free Encyclopedia: https://en.wikipedia.org/wiki/
2.   BibleGateway: https://www.biblegateway.com

Chapter 7   Gershom and Gershon

1.   BibleGateway: https://www.biblegateway.com
2.   Biblehub: https://www.biblehub.com

Chapter 8   69

1.   Wikipedia, The Free Encyclopedia: https://www. en.wikipedia.org/wiki/Gad
2.   BibleGateway: https://www.biblegateway.com
3.   Biblehub: https://www.biblehub.com

Chapter 9   Gedaliah and Gehazi

1.   BibleGateway: https://www.biblegateway.com
2.   Got Questions: https://gotquestions.org/Gedaliah-in-the-Bible.html
3.   Wikipedia, The Free Encyclopedia: https://www. enwikipedia.org/wiki

Chapter 10   The Mighty Warrior

1.   BibleGateway: https://www.biblegateway.com
2.   Biblehub: https://www.biblehub.com

Answers & Information Section

Chapter 7

"God is my help" is the meaning of the name Eliezer. Moses, the father of Gershom and Eliezer is one of the most well-known individual in the Bible, but relatively little is recorded about Gershom and Eliezer who were half Levite through their father and half Midianite through their mother.

Other Books by the Author:

From the Pew to the Pulpit   Published: 08/29/2007

Isaiah 26:3-4 "Perfect Peace"   Published: 09/07/2010

Isaiah 26:3-4 "Perfect Peace" The Last Single Digit   Published: 02/13/2012

Isaiah 26:3-4 "Perfect Peace III" Silver and Gold   Published: 10/24/2012

Isaiah 26:3-4 "Perfect Peace IV" The Kingdom Number   Published: 04/10/2013

Isaiah 26:3-4 "Perfect Peace V" 2541   Published: 09/06/2013

Isaiah 26:3-4 "Perfect Peace VI" Zacchaeus   Published: 02/28/2014

Isaiah 26:3-4 "Perfect Peace VII" Eleven   Published: 10/29/2014

Isaiah 26:3-4 "Perfect Peace VIII" Prayer   Published: 05/22/2015

Isaiah 26:3-4 "Perfect Peace IX" Sixteen   Published: 10/26/2015

Isaiah 26:3-4 "Perfect Peace X" Dreams   Published: 04/12/2016

Isaiah 26:3-4 "Perfect Peace XI" Door   Published: 02/13/2017

Isaiah 26:3-4 "Perfect Peace XII" River   Published: 08/02/2017

Isaiah 26:3-4 "Perfect Peace XIII" 1 Kings 19:1-18   Published: 12/18/2017

Printed in the United States
By Bookmasters